The MESSIAH

REVEALING JESUS
IN THE OLD TESTAMENT

CONCORDIA PUBLISHING HOUSE · SAINT LOUIS

Published by Concordia Publishing House
3558 S. Jefferson Avenue, St. Louis, MO 63118-3968
1-800-325-3040 • cph.org

Manufactured in the United States of America

1 2 3 4 5 6 7 8 9 10   31 30 29 28 27 26 25 24 23 22

Table of Contents

SESSION 1

❀ OPENING PRAYER ❀

Lord Jesus Christ, from the beginning, You have been with Your people, leading, protecting, forgiving, and guiding them. Give us Your Holy Spirit, that we may see You through the eyes of Your Old Testament people. Amen.

❀ INTRODUCTION

The Bible can be a tricky book to understand. Sometimes it helps to remember that the entire Old Testament was written in the BC years, and all the books in the New Testament were written in the AD years. But since that change from BC to AD occurred during Jesus' earthly life, we can get the impression Jesus wasn't around in Old Testament times. If that's the case, what sense is there in looking for Him in the Old Testament?

But listen to what Jesus told the people of Jerusalem about the Old Testament:

> **You search the Scriptures because you think that in them you have eternal life; and it is they that bear witness about Me.** (JOHN 5:39)

The reason Jesus could say this is because He is the almighty Son of God who was begotten in eternity, before God created the heavens and the earth. He has always existed and always will exist. He was not far off, watching human history unfold, waiting for His day in the sun;

indeed, He was active among His people throughout the entire Old Testament, as we will see in the pages of this book.

We will search through each Old Testament book to see where Jesus appears or where His life and work are predicted. But first, it will be helpful to get a firm grasp of Jesus' earthly life and mission. Then, as we work our way through the Old Testament, we will know to which part of His life and work the Old Testament writers were pointing.

The Life of Jesus

FROM ETERNITY

The Gospel of John opens with a beautiful reminder that Jesus Christ, the Son of God, was intricately involved when God created the heavens and the earth.

⊶ Read John 1:1–5.

The world was made through the Word, God's Son, and nothing was made without Him. But at the right time, that Word became human and dwelt among us.

Nazareth

GALILEE

CONCEPTION, BIRTH, AND CHILDHOOD

Luke 1 records the angel Gabriel's visit to the Virgin Mary, as he announced to her that she would conceive and bear God's Son. She was to name Him Jesus. Luke 2 records His birth in Bethlehem.

JUDEA

Jerusalem ●
Bethlehem ●

Jordan River

ISRAEL

⊶ Read Luke 2:1–7.

All the events in the Bible took place on this earth in historical time. By faith, we can go to those places and times in spirit and see them through the eyes of eyewitnesses whose testimony is recorded for us in the Scriptures. So it was with the earthly life of Jesus Christ. He was born at a specific time and place in human history, which is why Luke mentions specific details about Caesar's census. The Son of God was born in the town of Bethlehem, wrapped in swaddling cloths, and laid in a manger.

> *How does it transform our approach to Christmas when we realize the baby lying in the manger was actually the eternal Son of God, through whom everything was created?*

Jesus' childhood is recorded in Matthew 2 and Luke 2. After the Wise Men followed the star to Bethlehem, King Herod tried to kill the Christ Child. But having been warned in a dream, Joseph fled with Mary and Jesus to Egypt. After Herod died, Mary and Joseph made their way to Nazareth and raised Jesus there. Thus Jesus was known as "Jesus of Nazareth."

BAPTISM, TEMPTATION, AND GALILEAN MINISTRY

Matthew, Mark, and Luke each record Jesus going to the Jordan River to be baptized by John the Baptist when He was approximately thirty years old.

↔ Read Matthew 3:13–17.

> *Why is Jesus' Baptism so significant?*

In His Baptism, Jesus took on Himself all sins—including those that were washed from us at our Baptism—in preparation for carrying them to the cross to destroy them. He also was anointed with the

Holy Spirit to carry out His ministry. That is why we call Him the *Christ*, or "Anointed One."

His Baptism marked the beginning of Jesus' public ministry. He gathered twelve disciples and went throughout the villages and towns in the northern region of Galilee, teaching about God's kingdom, healing diseases, casting out demons, and raising the dead. Jesus worked most of His greatest miracles around the Sea of Galilee. Most of this ministry is recorded in Matthew, Mark, and Luke.

Judean Ministry

The Gospel of John records several events that occurred when Jesus brought His disciples to Jerusalem for various festivals. Most of these revealed the growing opposition He faced from the Jewish religious authorities.

Holy Week

All four Gospels record Jesus' last week on earth, which ended with His death and resurrection. Holy Week began with Jesus' triumphal entry into Jerusalem on Palm Sunday, as well as His teaching in the temple courts on Monday and Tuesday. Jesus' actions and teachings angered the Jewish leaders but delighted the crowds.

Late on Thursday of Holy Week, Jesus and His disciples gathered in an upper room to celebrate the Passover. At that Last Supper, He washed His disciples' feet, taught them about the Holy Spirit, and instituted the Sacrament of Holy Communion. After the meal, He led His disciples to the Garden of Gethsemane, where He prayed earnestly to the Father, finally submitting His will to His Father's will. Then He was betrayed by Judas, one of His twelve disciples. Jesus was arrested and led to the high priest's house.

Death

Jesus was tried by the Jewish high court and condemned early Friday morning for blasphemy (claiming to be the Son of God). The Jewish chief priests and religious leaders brought Him before the Roman governor, Pontius Pilate, for trial. Pilate declared Jesus not guilty of the charges against Him, but when pressured by the Jewish leaders and the crowds who were shouting for Jesus' death, Pilate condemned Jesus to execution by crucifixion. Roman soldiers led Jesus to Calvary, where He was crucified between two thieves. Jesus took our sins upon Himself, suffering and dying to satisfy God's wrath against us. His body was buried in a tomb. A large stone was rolled over the entrance, and a guard was set to prevent His disciples from stealing His body and claiming He had risen from the dead.

⤞ Read John 19:16–30.

What did Jesus mean when He said "It is finished" on the cross?

RESURRECTION

The following Sunday morning, Jesus rose from the dead. An angel came down from heaven and rolled the stone away from the tomb. When the guards saw the angel, they fell to the ground as if they were dead; then they fled the tomb and reported to the Jewish religious authorities, who bribed them to claim they had fallen asleep and the disciples had stolen Jesus' body.

The women followers of Jesus had gone to the tomb that morning to finish anointing His body, and they found the stone rolled away and the tomb empty. Two angels appeared, announcing that Jesus had risen from the dead. Jesus Himself appeared to His disciples several times over the next forty days.

ASCENSION

Forty days after rising from the dead, Jesus Christ ascended (rose up) into heaven, where He sits at God the Father's right hand, guiding everything that happens on earth for the good of His Church, and bringing our prayers to His heavenly Father. On the Last Day, Jesus will return to raise the dead, judge all people, and perfectly restore God's creation.

> *What parts of Jesus' life are most familiar to you? Which parts are a bit unclear?*
>
> ....
>
> ....

Our study through the Old Testament will help make all parts of Jesus' life, death, and resurrection more clear. But it also helps to read through the four Gospels and other New Testament books to gain a deeper understanding of and faith in Jesus' life and work.

With that basic outline of Jesus' life in place, we can now begin our search through the books of the Old Testament to identify where Christ is revealed to us and which parts of His mission are described.

Genesis

◇◇◇◇◇◇◇◇◇◇◇◇◇◇◇◇◇◇◇◇◇◇◇◇

In Genesis, Moses recorded beginnings—the beginning of creation, the beginning of sin, and the beginning of God unfolding His plan to save the world. We will see Jesus often in this book. Let's start in chapter 1 as God created the heavens and the earth.

❀ CREATION ❀

Genesis 1 describes how God created everything that exists today. It begins with the simple phrase "In the beginning, God created the heavens and the earth" (Genesis 1:1). In similar words, the Gospel of John shows us how Jesus, the eternal Son of God was involved.

In the beginning was the Word, and the Word was with God, and the Word was God. He was in the beginning with God. All things were made through Him, and without Him was not any thing made that was made. (John 1:1–3)

As you read the first chapter of Genesis, you read over and over again, "And God said . . ." Each of those statements refers to the Son of God, the mighty Word.

◦ Read about the creation of mankind in Genesis 1:26–31.

The participation of the Son and the Holy Spirit with God the Father in creation is clear in God's words "Let Us make man in Our image, after Our likeness" (Genesis 1:26). The fact that the Son of God actually became a human in history shines a light on the creation story and God's attitude toward His human creatures.

> *What difference does it make to you to know that Jesus was intimately involved in the creation of our world and the first humans?*

Because Jesus was creating the world at His Father's side, we know He is personally invested in our lives and in our world—because He made us and He made it. It also helps remind us about why He was willing to come into His world as a baby and go to such lengths as dying on the cross to save us from our sins and restore His creation.

❊ THE FIRST GOSPEL PROMISE ❊

Chapter 2 shows us how God created mankind, personally forming Adam's body from the earth, then breathing His own breath into his nostrils to make him a living being. God saw that it was not good for humans to be alone, so He took a rib from Adam's body and created a woman for him, then joined them in marriage. Adam and Eve lived in the Garden of Eden, surrounded by all kinds of beautiful trees filled with fruit to eat. Then we reach Genesis 3, where sin and death first invaded God's perfect creation.

◦ Read Genesis 3:1–15.

What was the serpent? Clearly it was not just another animal. It was an animal possessed by a fallen angel, known as Satan. The Bible gives us little information about how this angel turned evil and led a rebellion of angels against God. But he came to the Garden of Eden to turn the first humans against God as well.

He contradicted God's warning that eating the forbidden fruit would cause death, and he deceived the woman, Eve, into thinking God had withheld from her a great benefit that could be hers by eating the fruit. He promised her she would rise above the creaturely position God had given her and become like God.

But disobeying God did not bring the great joy Eve expected; instead, when she ate the fruit and gave it to her husband, Adam, and he ate it, it brought shame and guilt upon them both. Their disobedience brought suffering and death to them and to all God's creation. Now death casts such a shadow over each and every one of us that it seems like it is a natural part of earthly life. But God's Word reminds us that death and sin are foreign invaders. And now God's judgment would rest upon Adam and Eve and all of us, their offspring.

God would have been right and just to destroy Adam and Eve where they stood. But instead, for the sake of His Son, He was merciful and gracious to them—and to each of us. Knowing none of us can undo the damage we have done to ourselves, the world around us, and our relationship with Him, God set about to restore us Himself.

What solution did God declare for humanity's fall into sin?

Genesis 3:15 is the first prophecy of the salvation Jesus would accomplish on the cross. Thousands of years later, Jesus would be born of Mary, and when He was condemned and crucified, He would receive the punishment all of us deserve and would die in our place. His death would be torturous, burning like the venom of a serpent's bite—but in the process, He would "bruise the serpent's head"—He would inflict an eternally fatal injury. Even though we are still sinners, Jesus has destroyed Satan's power to accuse us of our sins and has set us free to live with God in glory forever. When Jesus returns to judge the world, Satan and his fallen angels will be banished to hell forever with unbelievers; and Jesus will restore His creation, and all believers will live with Him in glory in the new heavens and the new earth.

❀ NOAH AND THE FLOOD ❀

As we skim along through Genesis, we find Adam and Eve's children exhibiting the sinful nature they had inherited from their parents. Cain killed Abel because he was outraged that God accepted Abel's offering but not his own. When offered God's protection and forgiveness, Cain refused it and turned his back to live without God or His promised Savior. Cain's offspring followed his path, growing more heartless and cruel with each generation.

The promise of the coming Savior was carried by Abel's brother Seth and Seth's children. But as generations came and went, Seth's descendants were attracted to Cain's descendants. They intermarried, and most turned their backs on God and His promise of a Savior. The faithful remnant of Seth's descendants dwindled until only one family was left who worshiped God and believed His promise.

The next huge event takes place in chapters 6–9. Adam and Eve's descendants became so corrupt and filled the world with so much murder and violence that God regretted ever having created humans. He determined to destroy them in a worldwide flood. But God knew faithful Noah, a descendant of Seth, still believed by God's grace. God warned him of the coming flood and instructed him to build a giant ark, an oceangoing ship in which God would save that one human family and a small population of animals. The rest would be destroyed.

God waited patiently while Noah built the ark. Then He gathered together pairs of all the animal kinds and brought them to Noah, who loaded them safely into the ark. When God's time came, Noah and his family entered the ark, eight souls in all. God sealed them in, then sent the devastating flood that covered the entire earth, wiping out all land animals and humans who were outside the ark.

This teaches us something about Jesus Christ's return on Judgment Day. In Luke 17, Jesus compared the last day of the old world when

Noah entered the ark to the day He will return to judge the living and the dead, whom He will raise to life.

> **Just as it was in the days of Noah, so will it be in the days of the Son of Man. They were eating and drinking and marrying and being given in marriage, until the day when Noah entered the ark, and the flood came and destroyed them all. . . . So will it be on the day when the Son of Man is revealed.** (LUKE 17:26–27, 30)

Why should we see the story of the great flood and Noah's ark as more than a mythical children's story?

The fearful destruction of the ancient world is a startling foretaste of how it will be when Christ returns. Just as Noah and his family, who took refuge in the ark, were the only ones who escaped the floodwaters, only those who trust Jesus Christ as their Lord and Savior will be saved. All others will be wiped off the earth and suffer eternal torment in hell.

Jesus has built for us an "ark," His Holy Christian Church. Entering that ark by Baptism and God's Word, we can rest assured that we will be safe until Christ returns to judge the living and the dead and to cleanse and restore His entire creation.

❈ GOD CALLS ABRAM ❈

The flood removed unbelievers from the world, but it couldn't cleanse people's hearts of their sinful nature. Sadly, it didn't take long before Noah's sinful offspring again turned in unbelief from God, just as so many of Adam and Eve's descendants had. But instead of destroying the world again, God chose another man and his wife. From their descendants, He would raise up a nation in which He would preserve

His promise of a Savior, and in time, He would bring Jesus Christ into the world from that nation. The rest of Genesis is the story of this family.

↝ Read Genesis 12:1–3.

God made four promises to Abram:

1. God would make his descendants into a great nation.

2. God would bless him and make his name, or reputation, great.

3. God would bless those who blessed Abram and curse those who cursed him.

4. All the families of the earth would be blessed through him.

Where do we find the promise of the Christ in these three verses?

It was in the person of Abram's offspring Jesus Christ that all families of the earth would be blessed. On the cross, Jesus took the sins of every person upon Himself and won salvation for all people.

In chapters 12–18, we read how Abram and his wife, Sarai, left their native country and traveled through the land God promised to give their descendants. They lived in tents there, as strangers. But Abram built altars and called on the name of the Lord, who had appeared to him.

Abram faced moments of doubt and despair, especially as years passed and still the promised child did not come. After more than ten years passed, Sarai gave her maidservant Hagar to Abram to bear a child for her. Abram loved his son Ishmael, but God told him Ishmael would not be his heir; a child from Sarai's own body would be his heir.

❀ CHRIST APPEARS TO ABRAHAM ❀

Abram and Sarai waited twenty-four years, and near the end of that time, God renewed His promise and changed their names to Abraham and Sarah. And yet, Sarah still had not conceived the child God promised to give them. Then one day, three strangers appeared to Abraham in the heat of the day. Their visit demonstrated God's personal involvement in Abraham and Sarah's life and in the building of His nation.

⤙ Read Genesis 18:1–15.

While Abraham stood like a waiter before his three guests, ready to attend to their every need, one of them announced the time had come for Abraham and Sarah's promised son to be born. Sarah was listening nearby, inside the door of their tent. She heard the promise of the baby, and she laughed to herself.

Why did Sarah laugh at such good news?

God told Abraham to name their child *Isaac,* which means "he laughed." That name would always remind Abraham and Sarah of the great joy of their son's birth, but at the same time, it would constantly remind them of their own doubts, which God silenced by His almighty power.

Who were these three strangers? Clearly two of them were angels. They were later sent on ahead to bring Lot and his family out of Sodom and then destroy the city for its wickedness. The third was clearly the Lord. His words made clear that He was God—a truth Abraham came to see and believe by the time the two angels left for Sodom. Christ Himself had appeared to Abraham and talked with him.

❀ ABRAHAM OFFERS HIS SON ❀

Isaac was Abraham and Sarah's joy and delight. Imagine Abraham's shock the day God commanded him to sacrifice his dearly loved son.

⟶ Read Genesis 22:1–14.

Unlike Eve, who rose against God and His words, Abraham didn't bargain or look for a loophole. He immediately obeyed and went to do just as God had commanded him. He rose early the next morning, traveled three days, climbed the mountain with Isaac, and was ready to slay him—but then the Lord intervened.

> *How is this account similar to John 3:16, "God so loved the world, that He gave His only Son"?*

The sacrifice of Isaac introduced to the people of God a vivid, clearer picture of the Offspring of Eve who would crush the serpent's head. Like Isaac, Jesus would be the beloved Son of His Father. Like Isaac, Jesus would carry the wood of His sacrifice—the cross—up the mountain of sacrifice. But like the ram, Jesus would be sacrificed as a substitute for Isaac, for Abraham, for you and me, and for all humans. And just as the ram was caught by its horns in thorns, its head encircled by them, Jesus Christ would be sacrificed with a crown of thorns wrapped around His head.

❀ THE PATRIARCHS ❀

We use the term "patriarchs" to refer to Abraham, his son Isaac, grandson Jacob, and Jacob's twelve sons from whom God raised the promised nation. Jacob's twelve sons became the fathers of the twelve tribes of that chosen nation.

When Isaac was forty years old, his father provided for him a wife, Rebekah, from among Abraham's own relatives. God appeared to Isaac in a dream, promising to bless all nations through his descendant, the promised Christ. In time, Rebekah became pregnant with twin sons, Esau and Jacob. When she inquired of God, He told her both of her sons would become great nations, but the younger would be greater than the elder. The firstborn of the twins was Esau, and his younger brother was Jacob. The promised Savior would come from the family of Jacob.

Neither Esau nor Jacob seemed to be very spiritually minded. Esau was a hunter, very impulsive and flighty. One day, famished from hunting, he hastily sold his birthright to Jacob for a bowl of stew.

Later, as Isaac grew old and nearly blind, he sent Esau hunting, promising to give him a rich blessing when Esau returned and prepared supper for him. Rebekah overheard Isaac, and she plotted to deceive him so Jacob would receive the blessing God had promised him. Jacob resisted at first—not because he wanted to do what was right in God's eyes, but because he feared his father would discover the plot and curse him instead of bless him. But his mother convinced him and he did what she said, deceiving his father and stealing the blessing Isaac had planned to give Esau.

When Esau learned his brother had treacherously stolen his blessing, he plotted to murder him. Rebekah learned of his plot and convinced Isaac to send Jacob to her brother Laban to find a wife. Laban was as deceitful as Jacob had been. He promised to give his beautiful younger daughter Rachel to be Jacob's wife in exchange for Jacob working for him for seven years. Because of Isaac's blessing, Laban's flocks under Jacob's care multiplied greatly, making Laban wealthy.

Greedy Laban didn't want Jacob leaving after the seven years were over, so he deceived him under the cover of night by giving Jacob his older daughter, Leah, instead of Rachel. The next morning, Jacob was furious at his father-in-law's deceit. Laban insisted that it was the custom among his people to marry the oldest daughter first. He promised that for seven more years of labor, he would give Rachel to be Jacob's wife as well. Jacob accepted the deal.

A bitter jealousy grew between these sisters. When God saw that Leah was hated by Jacob and Rachel was favored, He closed Rachel's womb and gave Leah four sons. When Rachel saw that she was having no children, she gave her maidservant to Jacob to raise children through her. When this servant bore two sons, Leah gave *her* maidservant to Jacob, and *she* gave birth to two more sons. Then Leah had two more sons herself. Finally, God heard Rachel's prayer and gave her two sons.

From these two wives and their two maidservants, Jacob became the father of twelve sons. His fourth son, Judah, from Leah, was chosen by God to be the ancestor through whom the Christ would be born.

Jacob worked six more years to have his own flocks and herds. And though Laban changed Jacob's wages ten times, God protected Jacob and made him a wealthy man. Finally, after Jacob had lived with Laban for twenty years, God told him to return to Canaan, and He promised to protect him.

The night before Jacob met his brother, Esau, he sent messengers ahead who returned and told him Esau was coming with four hundred armed men. Jacob was terrified, thinking that his brother was still angry and was coming to murder him. So he sent ahead several groups of livestock as generous gifts for Esau, hoping to placate his brother and win his forgiveness before Jacob arrived with his wives and children. Then, all alone, he spent the night wrestling with a strange man whom he might initially have thought was Esau. But as the night wore on, he realized he was wrestling with the Lord Himself.

⚬ Read Genesis 32:22–32.

> *What made Jacob realize he was wrestling with the Lord Himself?*
>
> ....
>
> ....
>
> ....
>
> ....

The Son of God blessed Jacob and changed his name to *Israel* in Genesis 32:28. The next morning, Israel met his brother, Esau, who welcomed him back with joy and tears. Esau had not brought his four hundred men to kill Jacob but to protect him, his family, and his flocks and herds.

Jacob lived in Canaan as his father and grandfather had before him, building altars and calling on the name of the Lord.

Before we leave Genesis, we will look at one last person who foreshadowed the work of Jesus Christ. It is Jacob's eleventh son, Rachel's firstborn, Joseph.

❊ JOSEPH AND HIS BROTHERS ❊

Joseph's story is told in Genesis 37; 39–50. Remember that God had mercy on Rachel and opened her womb, so she gave Jacob a son in his old age. She named the son Joseph. Later, Rachel gave Jacob her second son, his twelfth, Benjamin; but she died in childbirth outside the town of Bethlehem.

Joseph was the firstborn of Jacob's deceased favorite wife, and Jacob favored him over his other sons. As a result, Joseph's older brothers resented and hated their half-brother. Once, while pasturing their family's flocks far from home, they saw Joseph coming to them across the hills. They plotted against him to kill him, but at the last moment, they changed their minds and sold him into slavery instead (Genesis 37). Joseph was taken to Egypt, where he became a slave to the captain of Pharaoh's guard in Egypt.

Joseph served conscientiously, and Potiphar, his master, came to see that he prospered greatly under Joseph's faithful care. He raised him above all the other slaves and made him steward of all his household. Joseph served faithfully, but Potiphar's wife became attracted to him. She tried day after day to seduce him, but Joseph refused.

Then one day when he and she were alone in the house, she grabbed him, and Joseph left his outer garment in her hands as he fled out of the house. She was so furious at being spurned that she told her husband his slave had tried to attack her and then had run away when she screamed. Potiphar had Joseph thrown into Pharaoh's dungeon.

But even in the dungeon, God blessed Joseph. His jailers realized he was faithful, and they entrusted him with more and more prisoners. When two of Pharaoh's officials, a baker and the cupbearer, angered their master, they were thrown into prison, where they were placed under Joseph's care. One night, both men had dreams. Joseph correctly interpreted both; the baker was executed and the cupbearer was restored to his position. But the cupbearer forgot about Joseph for two years, until Pharaoh himself had a bad dream.

God had given Pharaoh, king of Egypt, two horrifying images in a dream, which none of his wise men could interpret. Then the cupbearer remembered Joseph and advised the king to summon him. Joseph glorified God by saying he could not interpret the dream by his own wisdom or powers, but God would give Pharaoh the interpretation. Joseph told him the images in the dream were a divine warning to Pharaoh about an upcoming severe famine. There would be seven years of abundant harvests followed by seven years of famine that would devastate the country. He advised Pharaoh to store up extra grain in the coming good harvest years to feed and preserve Egypt through the famine.

Impressed by Joseph's ability to interpret his dream and the wise strategy he proposed, Pharaoh freed Joseph from prison and raised him to his right hand, giving him authority over all Egypt. Joseph oversaw the storing up of grain to save Egypt from the famine. And since the famine extended to the land of Canaan, Joseph was able to save his own family as well.

⋆ Read Genesis 45:1–15.

When Joseph's brothers came to Egypt to buy grain because of the famine, Joseph recognized them, but they did not recognize him.

21

He decided to test them to see if they regretted how they had mistreated him. He set up his full brother, Benjamin, Rachel's younger son, to make it look like he had stolen a silver cup. Joseph gave his brothers the chance to save themselves by sacrificing Benjamin, but none of them would do it. Judah himself begged Joseph to let him take Benjamin's place in prison, for he couldn't bear to see the sorrow that would fall upon his father, Jacob, if they returned without Benjamin. By this offer, Joseph knew his brothers were sincerely sorry for what they had done to him. He revealed himself to them, forgave them for their sins against him, and brought his whole family to Egypt to provide for them.

How was Joseph's story similar to the story of Jesus' life?

Just as Joseph was betrayed by his brothers and sold into slavery, Jesus was betrayed by His chosen disciple, Judas, and sold to the Jewish leaders. Just as Joseph was falsely accused by Potiphar's wife and unjustly punished, Jesus was falsely accused by the Jewish chief priest and leaders. Just as God raised Joseph from the dungeon to sit at Pharaoh's right hand, He raised Jesus from the dead and Jesus ascended into heaven to sit at the right hand of God the Father. And just as Joseph ruled all Egypt to preserve the nation and ultimately his own family, Jesus is ruling all of creation to preserve His Christian brothers and sisters.

❀ CONCLUSION ❀

Genesis closes with the children of the twelve tribes of Israel living in Egypt. They were eventually enslaved and remained there for 430 years, until God raised up Moses to bring them out of Egypt and take possession of the Promised Land. We will examine these events next time when we turn to the Book of Exodus.

❀ CLOSING PRAYER ❀

Lord Jesus Christ, thank You for creating our world and each of us with the Father and the Holy Spirit. Thank You for taking an active interest in our human family, delivering us through Noah and raising up Abraham and his descendants to be the nation from which You would enter human history as our Brother and Savior. Preserve us in this faith until the day You return to rule in the new heavens and the new earth forever. Amen.

SESSION 2

❁ OPENING PRAYER ❁

Lord Jesus Christ, today we look at Your work in the life of Moses about fifteen hundred years before Your birth. Give us great joy and confidence, knowing that You are with us as You were with Your people of old. Bless our study today by Your Holy Spirit. Amen.

❁ INTRODUCTION ❁

What is the first thing that comes to mind when you hear the words Exodus *and* Moses? *What, if anything, does this have to do with Jesus?*

In the last session, we searched the Book of Genesis to find hints of Jesus' life and His mission. All the events in that book took place about five hundred years before Moses was born. In this session, we will work through the events of Moses' lifetime, which are covered in the next four books he wrote: Exodus, Leviticus, Numbers, and Deuteronomy.

Exodus

⬦⬦⬦⬦⬦⬦⬦⬦⬦⬦⬦⬦⬦⬦⬦⬦

In Exodus, Moses recorded how God set free the descendants of Abraham, Isaac, and Jacob after 430 years of slavery in Egypt.

Session 1 explained how Israel became enslaved. Years after Joseph died, a new pharaoh rose to the throne who did not know all Joseph had done to save Egypt. He feared the growing number and power of the Israelites, and so he enslaved them.

❀ MOSES' BIRTH ❀

Despite their slavery, the Israelites kept growing in number and in power. Pharaoh and his people treated the Hebrew slaves heartlessly, but Israel kept growing more numerous. So Pharaoh tried to control Israel by commanding the Hebrew midwives to kill newborn baby boys, while baby girls were permitted to live. But the Hebrew midwives feared God more than Pharaoh, and they told Pharaoh the Israelite mothers were giving birth before they arrived. Then Pharaoh commanded all Hebrew male infants to be thrown into the Nile River. It was at this time that Moses was born.

⬥ Read Exodus 2:1–10.

God not only saved Moses' life but He also arranged for Moses to be raised and trained in the house of the Egyptian ruler himself.

> *How was Jesus' early life similar to that of Moses?*
>
> ....
> ....
> ....

The parallels between Moses' and Jesus' lives are amazing. When Moses was an infant, Pharaoh tried to kill him, along with all the other Hebrew baby boys. When Jesus was a young child, King Herod the Great tried to kill Him when he learned from the Wise Men that the promised King of Israel, a rival, had been born (see Matthew 2).

Moses was sheltered by Pharaoh's own daughter, who found him in a basket on the Nile, while Jesus also found shelter in Egypt.

❀ MOSES' FIRST FORTY YEARS ❀

Exodus does not reveal much about Moses' upbringing as a prince of Egypt. We only read that he was nursed by his Israelite mother, and when he was weaned,

> **she brought him to Pharaoh's daughter, and he became her son. She named him Moses, "Because," she said, "I drew him out of the water."** (EXODUS 2:10)

Oddly enough, we learn most about Moses' youth in Pharaoh's house in the New Testament account of the stoning of Stephen, the first Christian martyr. During Stephen's final speech, he told his prosecutors,

> **Moses was instructed in all the wisdom of the Egyptians, and he was mighty in his words and deeds.** (ACTS 7:22)

But Moses never forgot he was an Israelite. When he was forty years old, he tried to deliver an Israelite slave by killing the Egyptian who was whipping him. When his deed was discovered, he fled Egypt and wandered across the wilderness to Midian. He befriended the seven daughters of a Midianite priest who were watering their flocks. Moses married one of the daughters and shepherded his father-in-law's flocks for forty years. At the age of eighty, while his flocks were grazing near Mount Sinai, he noticed a bush burning on the mountain. He watched it carefully and saw that though it was burning, it was not consumed. So he went over to investigate.

↝ Read Exodus 3:1–12.

When God commanded Moses to return to Egypt and appear before Pharaoh, Moses was hesitant. He was probably afraid of what Pharaoh might do to him. He made excuses and claimed he was unable to speak clearly. So God told him his brother, Aaron, would be his spokesman. Finally, with all his excuses exhausted, Moses obeyed and set out for Egypt.

Moses and Aaron appeared before Pharaoh and commanded him to set Israel free. Not only did Pharaoh refuse to obey God his creator, but he also increased Israel's burden by forcing the Israelites to make bricks without providing the straw for them. They would have to go out at night to forage for straw, then make bricks by day. The Israelites reacted with grumbling and complaining, a tactic we will see repeatedly throughout the Books of Moses.

When Pharaoh refused to obey Moses, God afflicted Egypt with a series of ten plagues. These began as simple demonstrations of God's power, causing no lasting harm to Egypt. First, God turned the Nile River to blood; then He brought frogs up to fill the houses of the Egyptians. Next came gnats and flies; they were terrible nuisances for the Egyptians, but they didn't cause any lasting damage. But Pharaoh continued to harden his heart, refusing to free the Israelites.

So the Lord gradually intensified the plagues. The annoying plagues gave way to the destruction of Egypt's livestock, painful boils, and a plague of hail and fire that destroyed half of Egypt's crops. When Pharaoh still stubbornly refused to obey God, the Lord sent a plague of locusts that devoured whatever crops had survived the hail. Then, for the ninth plague, God enveloped Egypt in thick darkness for three days. This unnatural darkness reminds those familiar with Jesus' crucifixion of the three hours of darkness as Jesus hung from the cross.

When the sunlight returned, Pharaoh still refused to free Israel. So God sent His tenth and final plague in which His angel of death passed through Egypt, striking down all the firstborn males of people and animals. This event became known as the Passover.

❀ PASSOVER ❀

❧ Read Exodus 12:21–23, 28–36.

The key to the firstborn surviving the Passover was the blood of the Passover lamb spread across the doorways. This marked the difference not only between Israelites and Egyptians but also between believers in the God of Israel and unbelievers. Whenever the angel of death saw a house with the blood mark, he passed over that house and all the firstborn within were spared.

Passover was the pivotal event in the Old Testament and easily the greatest festival in the Israelite year—like our Christmas and Easter. Clear up to Jesus' time, Israelites from every nation gathered in Jerusalem to remember and celebrate God's great deliverance. Each annual Passover festival pointed back to that great deliverance. But even more important, it pointed straight ahead to a future, greater Passover, when Jesus Christ, the Savior promised to Adam and Eve, Abraham, Isaac, and Jacob, would shed His blood on the cross to free us from the angel of death on Judgment Day.

Around fifteen hundred years after the first Passover, Jesus was crucified at the time of the annual Passover celebration. In 1 Corinthians 5:7, Paul wrote, "Christ, our Passover lamb, has been sacrificed." In Baptism, we have been marked by His blood. When the angel of death approaches on Judgment Day, he will pass over each of us who is marked by Christ's blood.

How does Passover relate to Holy Communion?

After the final plague, Pharaoh drove Israel out of Egypt. The Egyptians were so glad to see Israel leave that they gave them gold, silver, bronze, and other precious things. But once the Israelites had gone, Pharaoh changed his mind and sent his army to recapture them. As Egypt's chariots and troops pursued the fleeing people of God, God opened a path through the Red Sea, allowing Israel to cross through it on dry ground. When the Egyptian army pursued them into the sea, God closed the waters in over them and the Egyptian army was destroyed.

From there, God led Israel to Mount Sinai, where Moses had seen the burning bush. When God came down to speak to Israel, the whole mountain was ablaze.

❀ THE TEN COMMANDMENTS ❀

On the appointed day, God came down on Mount Sinai in the sight of the Israelites. The mountain was covered in a thick cloud. There were earthquakes, thunder and lightning, and a loud trumpet blast. Then God's voice thundered each of the Ten Commandments:

1. You shall have no other gods before Me.
2. You shall not take the name of the Lord your God in vain.
3. Remember the Sabbath day, to keep it holy.
4. Honor your father and your mother.
5. You shall not murder.
6. You shall not commit adultery.
7. You shall not steal.
8. You shall not bear false witness against your neighbor.
9. You shall not covet your neighbor's house.
10. You shall not covet your neighbor's wife, or his male servant, or his female servant, or his ox, or his donkey, or anything that is your neighbor's. (See Exodus 20:3, 7, 8, 12–17.)

The Israelites were so terrified by God's mighty voice that they begged Moses to speak to God for them and tell them what God had commanded. They promised they would obey. This was pleasing to the Lord, so He summoned Moses to come up Mount Sinai into His presence.

Moses left Aaron in charge of the Israelites and, with his aide Joshua, he climbed Mount Sinai. There, he received God's rules for Israelite society and worship, instructions for how to construct Israel's worship space, and designs for garments the priests would wear when they offered the sacrifices.

❀ THE GOLDEN CALF ❀

Moses was on the mountain for forty days. When the people saw that he was not returning, they pressured Aaron to build them an idol.

Aaron had them bring the gold earrings, rings, and necklaces they had been given by the Egyptians. Then he melted these down and formed a golden calf. The Israelites held a feast and celebrated before the calf.

Moses heard the commotion, and God sent him down to stop His people. Moses was angry. He threw down the tablets on which the Commandments had been written and broke them at the foot of the mountain. He burned the gold and spread it in the water and made the Israelites drink it. Then he returned up the mountain for another forty days to plead with God to forgive Israel.

Moses' prayer for Israel was the next act that pointed ahead to Jesus very clearly.

✦ Read Exodus 32:30–35.

> *What offer did Moses make to turn God's anger from Israel?*
>
> ....
>
> ....
>
> ....
>
> ....

Moses' offer wonderfully foreshadowed Jesus' sacrifice on the cross. God would not accept Moses' offer because Moses was a sinner; his sacrifice was unacceptable. But Jesus was perfectly holy and innocent of any sin. On the cross, He carried our sins and was cursed and cut off from God. In that moment, God blotted Jesus' name out of His Book of Life and Jesus suffered the full wrath of God for our sins. When Jesus completed the payment for our sins, He cried out, "It is finished" (John 19:30). And then, reunited with His Father, His name firmly in the Book of Life once more, Jesus yielded up His life with the words "Father, into Your hands I commit My spirit!" (Luke 23:46).

❀ TABERNACLE ❀

At the close of Exodus, Moses related how God gave him designs for the tent of meeting and all its furnishings. The people of Israel constructed the tent of meeting and Moses assembled it. When it was completely set up, God's glorious cloud filled it. This brilliant cloud of God's glory would later appear to Jesus on the Mount of Transfiguration, when the glory of His divinity shone through His human body and the cloud of God the Father's glory overshadowed Him.

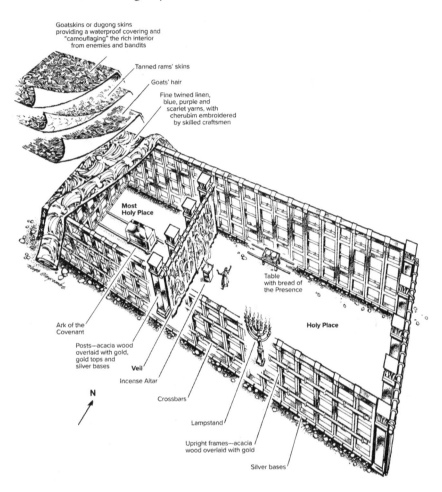

Goatskins or dugong skins providing a waterproof covering and "camouflaging" the rich interior from enemies and bandits

Tanned rams' skins

Goats' hair

Fine twined linen, blue, purple and scarlet yarns, with cherubim embroidered by skilled craftsmen

Most Holy Place

Table with bread of the Presence

Ark of the Covenant

Holy Place

Posts—acacia wood overlaid with gold, gold tops and silver bases

Veil

Incense Altar

N

Crossbars

Lampstand

Upright frames—acacia wood overlaid with gold

Silver bases

⤳ **Read Matthew 17:1–8.**

How was the tabernacle a foreshadowing of Jesus?

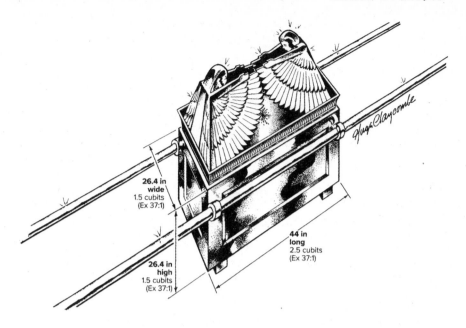

26.4 in
wide
1.5 cubits
(Ex 37:1)

44 in
long
2.5 cubits
(Ex 37:1)

26.4 in
high
1.5 cubits
(Ex 37:1)

In the physical "tent," or body, of Jesus Christ, God dwelt among His people, teaching and healing them, and saving us from our sins.

What is the connection between the mercy seat and the ark of the covenant?

The mercy seat represented God's presence among His people and symbolized Jesus, the only one through whom we have access to the Father. Only the high priest could enter the room that held the ark, but each Israelite could approach the ark from a distance by sacrificing at the bronze altar that stood outside the door of the tabernacle. This altar prefigured Christ's sacrifice on the cross by which our sins have been removed and we have access to God the Father.

Wherever Israel traveled through the wilderness, the ark of the covenant was with them, carried by Levites (members of the priestly tribe of Levi and cousins of Moses and Aaron).

Leviticus

As we move from Exodus to Leviticus, we find Israel and Moses still at Mount Sinai. During this time, God gave Moses the two replacement tablets with the Ten Commandments and all the instructions that make up the Book of Leviticus. This book was named for the tribe of Levi, from which Moses and Aaron were descended. In this book, God spelled out the responsibilities of the priests, who included Moses' brother, Aaron, and his descendants, and those of the Levites who would assist Aaron. This book provided instructions for the various sacrifices, feasts, and festivals, all of which pointed ahead in one way or another to the sacrifice Jesus later would make when He died in our place on the cross.

Besides describing the sacrifices and the functions of the priests, the Book of Leviticus tells us about a special festival called the Day of Atonement.

❈ SACRIFICES ❈

Leviticus gave specific instructions for six different sacrifices that offered forgiveness from various kinds of sins the Israelites might commit unintentionally.

The most frequently performed sacrifice was the burnt offering.

✤ Read Leviticus 6:8–13.
Like all sacrifices, the animal for the burnt offering was brought to the priest. The priest placed his hand on the animal's head and confessed the sins of the sinner or the sinful nation over it. This symbolized God transferring the guilt from the sinner to the sacrificial animal, which would die in the sinner's place. Then the sacrifice was killed and burned on the altar.

This sacrifice was made in the morning and in the evening, every single day. As soon as the ashes of the offering were removed, another animal replaced it, so there would continuously be a burnt offering on the altar.

What was the symbolism behind this sacrifice?

This same sacrifice was meant to be continuously burning on the altar, generation after generation, until Christ came. Then, for six hours (Mark 15:25, 33), Jesus would hang on the cross, paying the full debt and canceling all sins of all people of all time—for the same length of time the morning sacrifice burned upon the altar.

Each of the other offerings focused on the people's sins, which God forgave, and foreshadowed the payment Jesus made on the cross to forever satisfy God's wrath at each and every one of those sins for all people.

❀ HIGH PRIEST ❀

Our sin separates us from God. The tabernacle was set up to clearly portray that separation. Barriers were erected between the people and God, who dwelt in the tabernacle in the ark of the covenant.

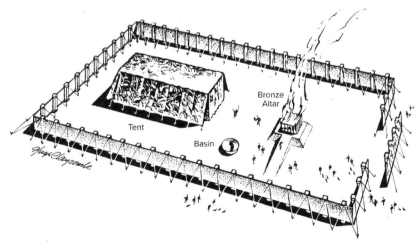

Gentile believers were restricted to the outermost court. Israelite women and children were restricted to the next court. Israelite men could gather in the courtyard outside the tabernacle itself. The tabernacle was divided into two rooms: the Holy Place and the Most Holy Place, where the ark of the covenant sat. Priests and Levites were the only Israelite men who could enter the Holy Place. And only the high priest could pass through the veil, or curtain, to enter the Most Holy Place, and then only on one day each year, the Day of Atonement.

⟶ Read Leviticus 16:11–19.

> *Why did God set such strict rules for how the high priest could approach His presence on the Day of Atonement?*
>
> _____
>
> _____
>
> _____
>
> _____
>
> _____

Each high priest represented Jesus Christ, the ultimate High Priest who brought His own blood before the Father in His death and permanently gained access to heaven for all believers. When Jesus died, the curtain of the temple dividing the Most Holy Place from the Holy Place split in two from top to bottom (Luke 23:45), signifying that Jesus had forever removed the barrier between God and sinners.

⟶ Read Hebrews 4:14–5:9.

> *How did Aaron and his sons, the line of high priests in Israel, foreshadow Jesus Christ?*
>
> _____
>
> _____
>
> _____
>
> _____
>
> _____

❀ DAY OF ATONEMENT ❀

On Mount Sinai, God established two festivals for Israel that pointed directly forward to Jesus' death on the cross. We have already looked at the spring festival called Passover. God also established a fall festival called the Day of Atonement. On the Day of Atonement, two goats were brought to the high priest. One was sacrificed and its blood collected in a bowl. The high priest carried this blood past the curtain and into the Most Holy Place in the tabernacle (later in Solomon's temple), stood before the ark of the covenant, and sprinkled the sacrificial blood on the mercy seat to atone for the people's sins. This pointed ahead to Good Friday, when our High Priest, Jesus, offered His blood to His heavenly Father to cleanse us from our sins.

The second goat was called the scapegoat, and it is the subject of the next reading.

❖ Read Leviticus 16:20–22.

The scapegoat revealed another glimpse into the saving work of Jesus Christ. This goat was not slain like other sacrifices. The priest laid his hand on the beast's head and confessed the sins of Israel, symbolically loading the goat with those sins. Then, as the people watched, the goat was led out into the wilderness and released, to carry their sins away into the wilderness.

How did the live goat point ahead to Jesus Christ?

Through Passover and the Day of Atonement, God gave Israel two opportunities each year to learn about and consider the salvation the coming Savior would accomplish by His death and resurrection. Consider this as you answer the next question.

> *What part of our worship service is most meaningful for you?*

Numbers

◇◇◇◇◇◇◇◇◇◇◇◇◇◇◇◇◇◇◇◇◇◇◇◇◇◇◇◇

From Leviticus, we move on to Moses' next book, called Numbers, named for two censuses he took of the Israelite warriors. The first took place right before the people left Mount Sinai, about a year after they left Egypt. God directed Moses to number the warriors in Israel. Afterward, He used His pillar of cloud and fire (Exodus 13:21) to lead them from Mount Sinai to the southern boundary of the Promised Land.

God's original plan was for Israel to spend a little over a year from the time they left Egypt until the time they entered and began to take possession of the Promised Land. When they arrived at the southern border, the people begged Moses to send spies to check out the land and gather information about the nations that possessed it and their defenses. Moses sent one spy from each of the twelve tribes of Israel.

Ten of the twelve were overwhelmed by the might of Canaan's inhabitants, who had built huge cities with massive walls to hold off invasion. These ten returned and gave a bad report about the land. They forgot all of God's mighty acts in Egypt and His promise to destroy the nations in Canaan. But two of the spies, Moses' aide, Joshua, and Caleb, from the tribe of Judah, reminded the people about God's power and protection. They encouraged the people to move forward and take the land. However, the people listened to the fearful ten and refused to obey God's command to go up and take possession. Instead, they complained that they would have been better off dying in Egypt or in the wilderness.

So God did as they wished. He sentenced the nation to wander for forty years, until all the fighting men of that generation had died in the wilderness. Their sons would replace them and go in and take possession of the land they had rejected. Of that earlier generation, only Joshua and Caleb, the two faithful spies, would enter the Promised Land. So, at God's command, Moses turned Israel aside and headed into what he described as a "great and terrifying wilderness" (Deuteronomy 1:19).

After Jesus' Baptism, He spent forty days in the wilderness being tempted by the devil. Jesus' answers to the three temptations of Satan that are recorded in Matthew and Luke came from the writings of Moses at the close of this forty years of wandering, in the Book of Deuteronomy.

> *Describe an opportunity you lost because you were filled with fear or doubt.*
>
> ....
>
> ....
>
> ....
>
> ....

Numbers shows us the faithless rebellions and complaining of the Israelites throughout these forty years. God used one of those incidents to reveal something about Jesus' coming salvation.

❀ THE BRONZE SERPENT ❀

❖ Read Numbers 21:4–9.

Throughout the pages of Numbers, we see numerous times when the Israelites grumbled about their situation—the situation they had brought upon themselves by their earlier disobedience at the southern border of the Promised Land. The plague described here was particularly severe, and God's solution was probably not popular. The people just wanted the snakes gone, but God provided a different solution, a solution that would test the faith of the afflicted Israelites. Would they be willing to believe God's promise when they looked at the bronze serpent hanging on a pole—or not?

> *How does the serpent on the pole foreshadow Jesus' mission?*
>
> ....
> ....
> ....
> ....
> ....

All of us descendants of Adam and Eve are infected with our sinful nature, the venom of the serpent who tempted Adam and Eve in the Garden of Eden. God raised up His Son on the cross, so that all who look to Him and trust God's promise to forgive their sin for Jesus' sake will be saved. Jesus referred to this event in John 3:14.

By the time Numbers closes, the forty years had ended. Israel was camped on the banks of the Jordan River, ready to cross over and enter the Promised Land. By God's mighty hand, they had conquered two mighty kings who had attacked them and they were now occupying those kings' lands. A second census of this new generation revealed that God had faithfully preserved Israel through the forty years in the wilderness.

Deuteronomy

The fifth and final Book of Moses is called *Deuteronomy*, which means "second law." Israel was on the eastern border of the Promised Land, waiting to cross the Jordan River. The older generation that had come out of Egypt were all dead except the two faithful spies, Joshua and Caleb. Before they crossed over into the Promised Land, Moses gave the children of Israel three farewell sermons, after which he died. God raised up Joshua to lead the people into the Promised Land.

In the first sermon, Moses taught the people where to find courage to face the powerful enemies awaiting them in Canaan. They were to recall God's faithfulness in bringing them out of Egypt, leading and providing for them through the wilderness years and defeating the two powerful kings east of the Jordan River. Moses assured them that God would faithfully bring them into the Promised Land and give them victory over the Canaanites.

Name a great work of God in the Bible that gives you comfort and confidence when you face difficulties.

In the longer second sermon, Moses taught Israel about their life under God's covenant, the rules that would guide their lives together as God's people in the Promised Land.

❈ LESSONS FROM DEUTERONOMY ❈

After Jesus was baptized, He was led by the Spirit into the wilderness to fast for forty days and be tempted by Satan. During this time, He referred to Moses' teachings in Deuteronomy to answer Satan's cunning temptations.

When Satan challenged Jesus to prove He was the Son of God by turning rocks into bread, Jesus referred to Deuteronomy 8:2–3:

And you shall remember the whole way that the LORD your God has led you these forty years in the wilderness, that He might humble you, testing you to know what was in your heart, whether you would keep His commandments or not. And He humbled you and let you hunger and fed you with manna, which you did not know, nor did your fathers know, that He might make you know that *man does not live by*

bread alone, but man lives by every word that comes from the mouth of the LORD. [EMPHASIS ADDED]

How does this passage fit with Jesus' forty days of fasting in the wilderness?

Then Satan took Jesus to the highest point of the temple and told Him to throw Himself off, even quoting Psalm 91 about God sending His angels to "bear [Him] up" in their hands. Jesus answered with Deuteronomy 6:16, **"You shall not put the Lord your God to the test."** These words were originally spoken at Massah, between Egypt and Mount Sinai, where the Israelites grumbled about being without water and questioned if God was with them or not.

How was Jesus' situation on the peak of the temple similar to Israel's experience at Massah?

Satan's third temptation came on a high mountain, where he showed Jesus the kingdoms of the world and all their glory. He offered to give them to Jesus if He would bow down and worship him. In His answer, Jesus again quoted words from the Book of Deuteronomy:

When the LORD your God brings you into the land that He swore to your fathers, to Abraham, to Isaac, and to Jacob,

to give you—with great and good cities that you did not build, and houses full of all good things that you did not fill, and cisterns that you did not dig, and vineyards and olive trees that you did not plant—and when you eat and are full, then take care lest you forget the LORD, who brought you out of the land of Egypt, out of the house of slavery. *It is the LORD your God you shall fear. Him you shall serve and by His name you shall swear. You shall not go after other gods, the gods of the peoples who are around you* (DEUTERONOMY 6:10–14, EMPHASIS ADDED)

How did Jesus use this passage to resist Satan's shortcut?

❀ A PROPHET LIKE ME ❀

Included in this section are two teachings of Moses that pointed directly to Jesus. The first is about a prophet like Moses whom God would raise up from His people. The Bible points out how unique Moses was among the prophets in Israel. When Aaron and Miriam, Moses' brother and sister, grumbled against his leadership, God appeared to them and pointed out,

If there is a prophet among you, I the LORD make Myself known to him in a vision; I speak with him in a dream. Not so with My servant Moses. He is faithful in all My house. With him I speak mouth to mouth, clearly, and not in riddles, and he beholds the form of the LORD. Why then were you not afraid to speak against My servant Moses?
(NUMBERS 12:6–8)

This passage speaks volumes when we listen to the next prophecy.

⚬ Read Deuteronomy 18:15–19.

Many great and famous prophets followed Moses: Samuel, David, Elijah, Elisha, Isaiah, Jeremiah, Ezekiel, and Daniel. Yet none of these rose to the level of Moses.

> *How does this promise relate to Jesus?*

In John 14:24, Jesus mentions that the words He spoke were not His own but the words of His Father who sent Him. Also, at Jesus' transfiguration, God the Father commanded His disciples Peter, James, and John to "listen to Him" (Matthew 17:5)—just as Moses commanded here.

❀ A MAN HANGED ON A TREE IS CURSED ❀

⚬ Read Deuteronomy 21:22–23.

In Deuteronomy 21, Moses laid out miscellaneous rules for Israel. This one stated that in God's eyes, a person who was hanged was cursed. If his dead body remained hanging on a tree after he died, the land itself would fall under that curse.

> *How does this passage point ahead to Jesus?*

Jesus was punished for our sins and died that afternoon. The Jewish leaders were careful to obey Moses' command and ensure that Jesus and the thieves crucified with Him died and were removed from their crosses and buried before night fell.

❀ CONCLUSION ❀

Deuteronomy closes with Israel ratifying their covenant, agreeing to live in fear, love, and trust toward God while loving one another as themselves. Moses handed the leadership over to Joshua, then climbed Mount Nebo, where God showed him all of the Promised Land. There Moses died, and God buried him.

> *What new thing have you learned from this section that helps you better understand Jesus as He is presented in the Old Testament?*

❀ CLOSING PRAYER ❀

Lord Jesus Christ, through Your servant Moses, You delivered Israel from slavery in Egypt and established them as Your own nation. Thank You for dying on the cross to deliver us from slavery to sin, death, Satan, and hell, and for rising to gather us as Your own people and lead us to the promised land of heaven. Give us grace to trust in You at all times and follow You without grumbling and unbelief as You lead us day by day. Amen.

SESSION 3

❀ **OPENING PRAYER** ❀

Lord Jesus Christ, today we see how You brought Your people into the Promised Land and kept reaching out to them every time they strayed. Forgive us the times we stray from You, and guide us by Your Spirit that we may praise You for Your faithfulness and salvation. Amen.

❀ **INTRODUCTION** ❀

In the last session, we found references to Jesus' life and work as we studied the life of Moses in his books of Exodus, Leviticus, Numbers, and Deuteronomy. Next we will begin exploring a group of books that trace the history of God's nation, Israel. They are the first of the Old Testament's Historical Books. These books show us how God preserved the line that would lead to the birth of His Son, our Savior. At the same time, He also preserved the transmission of His faith-creating promise to His people and expanded it with further details. We continue with Joshua, who was Moses' aide and who commanded Israel's army when it went into battle. He was the leader God chose to succeed Moses and lead Israel into the Promised Land.

Joshua

It is likely that Joshua wrote most of the book that carries his name. His book explains how God brought His people Israel into the Promised

Land, where the Savior of the world would be born. Joshua describes how the Lord led him to defeat thirty-one kings and their heavily fortified cities.

Before reading a single verse of this book, we have encountered Jesus. We see Him in the name *Joshua*. *Joshua* is the English rendering of the Hebrew name that means "the Lord saves." Other Old Testament forms of the name include *Hosea* and *Isaiah*. The Greek form of the name is rendered in English as *Jesus*.

Besides having the same name in common, both leaders conquered God's enemies. Joshua conquered thirty-one Canaanite kings. Jesus conquered the devil, sin, death, and hell by His death and resurrection. In addition, both brought God's people safely into the Promised Land—Joshua led Israel into Canaan, and Christ Jesus leads all believers into God's presence in the new heavens and the new earth.

But even beyond this, the book contains several references to Christ and an appearance by the preincarnate Christ Himself.

❊ RAHAB THE PROSTITUTE ❊

At the beginning of the book, Israel is camped along the east bank of the Jordan River, with the Promised Land lying across the river to the west.

In chapter 2, we read that Joshua sent two spies to view the land along the river, especially Jericho, the strongly fortified city that secured the Canaanite frontier to the west of the Jordan. Any invasion of the Promised Land had to begin with Jericho.

The spies snuck into Jericho and stayed with a woman of the city named Rahab. Not only was she a Gentile, but she was also a prostitute, whose house was built into Jericho's city wall. When the leaders of Jericho got word that two spies were in Rahab's house, they told her to bring them out. Rahab said they had been there but had left Jericho to return to Israel. While the guards went searching outside the city walls, she hid the spies on her roof, protecting them and revealing her faith in Israel's God.

❧ Read Joshua 2.

It is astounding that the people in Jericho were still talking about the ten great plagues in Egypt and the way the God of the Israelites had brought His people through the Red Sea and drowned the Egyptians who rode in after them. Those events had occurred forty years before, yet they filled the hearts of the people of Jericho with great fear. But God used these same mighty acts to create faith in the heart of this Canaanite, this Gentile prostitute.

Before we go any further with Rahab's story, you may wonder, what in the world does a Canaanite prostitute have to do with Jesus? In addition to believing in God and protecting Israel's spies, her biggest contribution is found in the list of Jesus' ancestors, which we read in Matthew 1:

> Salmon [was] the father of Boaz by *Rahab*, and Boaz
> the father of Obed by Ruth, and Obed the father
> of Jesse, and Jesse the father of David the king.
> (MATTHEW 1:5–6, EMPHASIS ADDED)

Why is Rahab's presence in the line of Jesus so important?

The fact that God included a Gentile prostitute in Christ's family tree indicates the universal scope of the salvation Jesus won. He offers salvation to all who believe, no matter who they are, where they come from, or what they have done.

In return for protecting the spies from the people of Jericho, Rahab asked that they protect her and her family from destruction when they returned to capture Jericho. The spies gave her a scarlet cord and told her to tie it in the window of her house. Everyone in her house would be spared, but any who wandered outside would suffer destruction with the rest of Jericho.

❀ COMMANDER OF THE LORD'S ARMY ❀

Encouraged by the spies' report and Rahab's testimony, the Israelites set out to cross the Jordan River. Though the river was at flood stage, God told Joshua to command the priests carrying the ark of the covenant to step down into the Jordan. As soon as the priests set foot in the waters, the Jordan stopped flowing and Israel crossed over on dry land.

Joshua ordered the young men to take twelve stones from the dry riverbed and carry them up onto the bank, where they would serve as a memorial for all future generations. When all Israel had crossed over, the river returned to its channels, and whatever courage had remained in the people of Jericho melted away completely.

God commanded Joshua to circumcise the men of Israel, and a fascinating event took place while they stayed in camp to heal. As Joshua was preparing Israel for war, he met a man standing before him, holding a drawn sword in his hand.

↝ Read Judges 5:13–15.

Who was this man?

Consider the clues we are given:

1. He commanded the army of the Lord.
2. Joshua worshiped him and called him "my lord."
3. He commanded Joshua to remove his sandals, just as the Lord had commanded Moses at the burning bush.
4. His presence made the ground holy.

He could be none other than the Christ Himself, present with His people and ready to lead the angel armies against Israel's enemies. This position of Jesus as commander of the angel armies pointed ahead to an important event in Jesus' life.

You may recall that when Jesus was arrested, Peter drew his sword to protect Jesus and struck the servant of the high priest, cutting off his ear. Jesus told Peter to put away his sword and asked him if he didn't realize that Jesus could call upon the Father and He would send Him twelve legions of angels. But if He did that, how would the Scripture be fulfilled that said He would sacrifice Himself for the sins of the world?

Jesus was right there with Joshua and the people of Israel. He is also with us constantly, with all His angel armies ready to defend His children against Satan and all our enemies. He will also appear with all these angels in great glory when He returns to judge the world. He will command these same angel armies to gather all people from every part of the world and bring us before His throne for judgment. Believers will be gathered with Christ to share eternity in the newly restored creation, while unbelievers will be punished in hell with the fallen angels forever.

The rest of the Book of Joshua records the military victories God gave Joshua and Israel, often through amazing miracles. Two of these miracles in a single battle stand out as great acts of God that pointed ahead to Jesus' life and ministry.

❀ THE SUN STANDS STILL ❀

↝ Read Joshua 10:1–15.

> *What great miracles did God work? Why?*
>
> _____
>
> _____
>
> _____
>
> _____
>
> _____

Jesus also worked many miracles that demonstrated His divinity. These included stilling storms on the Sea of Galilee, walking on water, and an innumerable array of healing miracles.

With God's help, Joshua defeated thirty-one kings. He and the tribal leaders divided the land among the tribes of Israel. It wasn't the entire territory God had promised Israel. That would have to wait until each tribe grew strong enough to drive out the remaining Canaanites and possess their territory.

The Book of Joshua reminds us of the future, when Jesus Christ will return with His angel armies. He will drive Satan, his evil angels, and all unbelievers from the earth. Then He will restore creation to perfection, and we will live with Him in glorified bodies, in the promised land of the new heavens and the new earth, forever.

Judges

We do not know with certainty who wrote Judges, but many scholars think it was the judge and prophet Samuel. Judges marks a perilous time, the four hundred years after Joshua conquered the Promised Land.

At the close of the Book of Joshua, the strength of the Canaanites was broken, but there was still some mop-up work for the tribes to do to drive out the remaining Canaanites and take possession of their entire territory. But even though each tribe grew stronger and more numerous in the following years, they failed to drive out the remaining Canaanites. Instead, the Israelites became curious about the gods of the Canaanites and how the people served them. Israel even began worshiping the Canaanites' false gods—despite the fact that these gods had been unable to defend the Canaanites against Israel's God!

The twelve tribes fell into disobedience and idolatry. Though His people were unfaithful, God faithfully preserved the line leading to Christ and safeguarded His promises of the Savior's coming.

In Deuteronomy, Moses had warned the tribes that if they turned from God's covenant with them and worshiped false gods, He would deliver them into the hands of foreign kings. And that is exactly what happened to Israel. Again and again when they rebelled against God, the Lord brought in foreign invaders, who oppressed them and made their lives miserable.

Whenever Israel finally remembered God and cried out to Him in their misery, God would faithfully raise up a deliverer for them, a judge. As long as the judge lived, Israel served God. But after the judge died, they quickly abandoned God again, beginning a new cycle of captivity and prayers for deliverance. The Book of Judges presents a long parade of judges. Sadly, the nation kept spiraling further and further away from God. One of the more famous judges was a man named Gideon.

❀ GIDEON ❀

Four judges had already come and gone. When Israel turned away yet again, God brought the people of Midian upon them. The Midianites brought along all their livestock to devour all of Israel's crops from their fields, leaving no food for Israel and its livestock. This drove the Israelites to go up into the mountains, caves, and strongholds to hide. For seven years, Israel suffered; then they finally cried out to God once more, and He called Gideon to deliver them.

⊸ Read Judges 6:11–24.

> *Why was Gideon an unlikely judge?*

If you look at Gideon's call, you see another mysterious figure. Was the being speaking to Gideon an angel? Notice particularly verse 14: "And the LORD turned to him and said . . ." An angel would never be called "the LORD," the "I AM." Once again, we are seeing the preincarnate Christ as the Angel of the Lord who appeared to Gideon. Read those verses again, keeping in mind that it is Jesus speaking with Gideon.

Gideon is famous for demanding signs from the Lord. He laid out a fleece and asked God to let dew fall on the fleece alone and not on the ground. And it was so. The next night, Gideon asked God to have the dew fall on everything *but* the fleece and keep the fleece dry. God patiently did that as well.

Reassured by God's signs, Gideon finally obeyed the Lord's command to lead a tiny force of three hundred men into battle, completely unarmed. In one hand, they held a trumpet, and in the other, a torch hidden in a jar. In the middle of the night, at Gideon's command, they broke the jars; held up their torches; shouted, "A sword for the LORD and for Gideon!"; and then blew their trumpets. In the din and confusion, God caused the Midianite warriors to fall into a panic and slaughter one another.

Gideon gathered all the Israelites who were willing to pursue the enemy. By the end of the battle, God had delivered Israel out of the hand of the Midianites.

❋ SAMSON ❋

Of all the judges, Samson stands out as one of the biggest wastes in the history of God's people. Gifted by the Holy Spirit with incredible, superhuman strength, he used it only to satisfy his own sinful lusts and petty temper. He had no concern for holiness or for the people of God and their needs. In many ways, he was the exact opposite of Jesus Christ.

Consider Samson's feats of strength:

- He killed a lion with his bare hands.
- He struck down thirty Philistines.
- He slew a thousand Philistines using only the jawbone of a donkey.
- He tore out the doors of the gate of a city with its two posts and bars; then, putting them on his shoulders, he carried them up to the top of a hill, where he set them in place.

But Samson was arrogant, thinking the strength was his and forgetting that it was actually a gift from God. He later fell in love with a Philistine woman. When he confided in her, she betrayed him by cutting off his hair, which broke his vow to the Lord. This caused the Spirit of the Lord to depart from him—and with the Spirit gone, Samson's great strength left him too. The Philistines blinded Samson and bound him in bronze shackles.

❧ Read Judges 16:23–27.

Samson stands in stark contrast to Jesus Christ, motivated as he was by selfish desires, while Christ was entirely selfless throughout His earthly life. Yet they did share some things in common:

- Both battled God's enemies single-handedly without raising armies.
- Both were captured, bound, and mocked.
- Both delivered God's people in their deaths.

> *How did Samson free Israel from their captivity to the Philistines?*

Of course, in Jesus' death on the cross, He vanquished Satan, sin, death, and hell for all believers.

Sadly, as the Book of Judges moves on toward its conclusion, the people of Israel continued drifting further and further from the Lord. Their behavior is best summed up in the closing verse of the book:

In those days there was no king in Israel. Everyone did what was right in his own eyes. (JUDGES 21:25)

But even this sad condition of Israel pointed ahead to the world in which Jesus appeared in the flesh:

When He saw the crowds, He had compassion for them, because they were harassed and helpless, like sheep without a shepherd. (MATTHEW 9:36)

[Jesus said,] I was sent only to the lost sheep of Israel. (MATTHEW 15:24)

Ruth

◇◇◇◇◇◇◇◇◇◇◇◇◇◇

We do not know who wrote the Book of Ruth. Its events took place during the time of the judges, and it reveals how God preserved the line leading to the promised Savior despite Israel's unfaithfulness. Where the Book of Judges focuses on the faithless nation, Ruth focuses on a family that remained faithful by God's grace.

Ruth was a woman of Moab (descended from Abraham's nephew Lot) who had married an Israelite man. Her husband was sojourning in Moab with his parents and brother because of a famine in their hometown of Bethlehem. While in Moab, Ruth's husband died, as did his brother and father. When Ruth's mother-in-law, Naomi, learned God had granted relief to Israel, she set out to return to Bethlehem. She tried to convince her two widowed daughters-in-law to stay in Moab and find husbands. But Ruth clung to her, ready to go and live the life of a poor widow under the protection of Naomi's God.

⮞ Read Ruth 1:15–18.

When they reached Bethlehem, Naomi sent Ruth to the neighbors' fields to gather food. Ruth found herself in the fields of a relative of her late husband whose name was Boaz. Boaz was a good and noble man who feared God. He protected Ruth, provided for her and Naomi, and promised to redeem Naomi's property and take Ruth as his wife.

❈ BOAZ — THE KINSMAN-REDEEMER ❈

❖ Read Ruth 4:1–12.

> *What is a redeemer?*
>
> _____
> _____
> _____
> _____

Boaz bought back the property of Naomi's husband and two sons, and he married Ruth. Notice the good wishes of the townspeople toward Ruth and the offspring she would bear Boaz.

❈ GENEALOGY ❈

Read Ruth 4:13–17.

> *Why is the Book of Ruth important enough to be in the Bible?*
>
> _____
> _____
> _____
> _____

Ruth and Boaz were ancestors of Israel's great King David. But even more important than her relationship to King David was the fact that Ruth joined the family line leading through David to Jesus Christ. Back in Judges, we met Rahab, the Canaanite from Jericho who had joined Jesus' line. She was an ancestor of Boaz. Like Rahab, Ruth was not an Israelite. But God brought this believing Moabite not only into Israel but also into the line that led to Israel's promised Savior, Jesus Christ.

There's one more interesting connection to Jesus Christ: all the action in Ruth 2–4 took place in Jesus' birthplace, the little town of Bethlehem.

1 Samuel

◇◇◇◇◇◇◇◇◇◇◇◇◇◇◇◇◇◇◇◇◇◇◇◇◇◇

The early chapters of 1 Samuel were most likely written by Samuel himself. After his death (recorded in chapter 25), an anonymous author continued the writing; it was most likely a successor of Samuel. The events of 1 Samuel mark the end of the period of the judges and the beginning of the kingdom of Israel. Through it all, God preserved the line of the Savior and strengthened Israel to share His promise of salvation with neighboring nations. In 1 Samuel, we see the transition from judges ruling Israel to a king.

The same spiritual decline evident throughout the Book of Judges marks the beginning of 1 Samuel, when God raised up the last judge— Samuel himself—to stop the decline.

❀ SAMUEL'S BIRTH ❀

In the Bible, it often seems that special servants of God have unique stories surrounding their birth. Isaac was a miracle child born to Sarah, who had not conceived a child during her childbearing years and was well past menopause. John the Baptist was born to Zechariah and Elizabeth, who likewise had not conceived a child before she was too old to do so naturally. It was almost as if the long wait for pregnancy marked that miracle child as something special.

Samuel's birth was similar. His mother, Hannah, had been unable to have children. She wasn't past the normal age of bearing children, as Sarah and Elizabeth were, but she was barren. Chapter 1 records for us her fervent prayer to the Lord.

❧ Read 1 Samuel 1:9–20.

What promise did Hannah make to the Lord regarding her son?

....

....

....

God granted Hannah's prayer, and she gave birth to Samuel. When she had weaned him, she kept her promise, bringing him to the tabernacle, which was then set up at Shiloh. She left Samuel with Eli, the high priest who had spoken to her in chapter 1.

Hannah broke out in a prayer of thanksgiving that shares many themes with the prayer the Virgin Mary spoke when she was pregnant with Jesus Christ.

↪ Read 1 Samuel 2:1–10.

> *How was Hannah's prayer similar to Mary's song in Luke 1:46–55?*

Samuel was a young man when God called him to service as a prophet, a mouthpiece who brought God's message to His people.

↪ Read 1 Samuel 3:1–21.

> *How are verses 19–20 similar to Luke 2:52, "And Jesus increased in wisdom and in stature and in favor with God and man"?*

Shortly after God called Samuel, He gave Samuel a warning concerning the high priest, Eli, and his wicked sons, who were priests but badly misused their office. Eli's sons carried the ark of the covenant up out of the tabernacle into a battle against the Philistines. The sons were killed, the army of Israel was defeated, Shiloh was obliterated, and the ark was captured. When Eli heard the news about the ark, he fell over backward, broke his neck, and died.

Meanwhile, the Philistines celebrated their victory by bringing the ark into the temple of their god Dagon. The next morning, Dagon's priests found the idol had fallen on its face before the ark. They set it back upright, but the next morning, they found it had fallen again, and this time its head and hands had broken off. God afflicted the Philistines with terror and tumors until seven months later, when they returned the ark to Israel.[1]

Samuel grew to be an adult. His reputation as a prophet and priest grew throughout Israel, and he became the last judge of Israel.

❀ SAMUEL—PROPHET, PRIEST, AND RULER/JUDGE ❀

⤙ Read 1 Samuel 7:3–13.

> *How was Samuel unique among the judges?*
>
> ....
>
> ....
>
> ....

As Israel's prophet, priest, and judge, Samuel was a model of Jesus Christ, who is our Prophet, Priest, and King. As Prophet, Jesus brought God's message to us.

Jesus answered them, "My teaching is not Mine, but His who sent Me." (JOHN 7:16)

As Priest, Jesus offered Himself up as the sacrifice for our sins.

But when Christ appeared as a high priest of the good things that have come, then through the greater and more perfect tent (not made with hands, that is, not of this creation) He

---

1 Interestingly, the ark was never returned to the tabernacle. It remained in Kiriath-jearim until David brought it up to Jerusalem. The tabernacle and its other furnishings were moved from Shiloh to Gibeon, where Solomon later prayed for wisdom and discretion. The ark and the other worship items were not reunited until Solomon built the temple and brought them together again.

entered once for all into the holy places, not by means of the blood of goats and calves but by means of His own blood, thus securing an eternal redemption. (HEBREWS 9:11–12)

And as King, He sits at God the Father's right hand, ruling all nations for the benefit of His Church.

And Jesus came and said to them, "All authority in heaven and on earth has been given to Me." (MATTHEW 28:18)

Samuel ruled Israel wisely. But when he grew old, he made his sons priests, and they became corrupt. The Israelites recognized this and demanded that he appoint a king for them.

❁ KING SAUL ❁

Israel grew tired of being ruled by judges because after each judge died, it found itself overrun by foreign nations. The people failed to realize that their own idolatry and sin were the cause. They thought it was because they lacked a strong centralized government, which in that day meant a king and his descendants.

They demanded that Samuel appoint a king for them, and God gave them what they asked. God selected Saul of the tribe of Benjamin to be Israel's first king, and Samuel anointed him. Samuel stopped being Israel's judge, but he continued as its prophet and priest.

Saul began his reign as a humble man full of the Holy Spirit because of Samuel's anointing. God worked great victories through him over Israel's enemies. But over time, he became proud and arrogant and was not careful to do everything God commanded him. As one battle drew near, he decided to take upon himself the office of priest, which God had not given him; that still belonged to Samuel.

❖ Read 1 Samuel 13:8–14.

What was so bad about Saul offering the sacrifice, since Samuel was late?

When Saul saw his troops abandoning him in fear, he became impatient. He revealed his distrust of both Samuel and God. Only priests were authorized to make sacrifices, but Saul thought he needed to take matters into his own hands before he lost his whole army. The problem was, even after he made this unlawful sacrifice, Saul's army still fled. In the end, he found his forces reduced to a mere six hundred men. And all of these were unarmed except for Saul and his son Jonathan, both of whom had armor and weapons.

In a sense, Saul shows Jesus in an opposite light. Whereas Saul took matters into his own hands, Jesus completely trusted His Father. When Jesus had fasted forty days and was very hungry, Satan tempted Him to take matters into His own hands and tell the stones to become bread to save Himself. But Jesus showed His patience and faith: "It is written, 'Man shall not live by bread alone, but by every word that comes from the mouth of God'" (Matthew 4:4).

Actually, Saul's son Jonathan was a man of much greater faith than his father. Jonathan trusted God so much that he singlehandedly destroyed a Philistine garrison, a deliverance similar to David defeating Goliath.

But despite his son Jonathan's example, Saul did not learn his lesson. He became even more arrogant and proud, disobeying God's commands that came to him through Samuel.

Finally, God rejected Saul, withdrawing His Holy Spirit and directing Samuel to anoint a replacement king—David of Bethlehem, descendant of Ruth and Boaz.

❈ DAVID AND GOLIATH ❈

When Samuel anointed David, God filled the young shepherd with His Holy Spirit. Now David demonstrated faith and courage, which Saul completely lacked without the Holy Spirit empowering him.

❧ Read 1 Samuel 17:38–50.

> *How does David's battle against Goliath foreshadow Jesus' battle with Satan?*
>
> _____
>
> _____
>
> _____
>
> _____
>
> _____

But through these two unlikely heroes from Bethlehem, God delivered His people.

After delivering Israel from Goliath, David faithfully served Saul as a commander in Israel's army, and eventually he was promoted to the trusted position of captain over Saul's bodyguard. But Saul grew jealous of David's popularity and paranoid that David would rise against him. So he used Israel's army to hunt David down and pursue him, as recounted throughout the remainder of 1 Samuel.

⤝ Read 1 Samuel 23:15–29.

> *How was David's experience with Saul's jealousy similar to what Jesus later experienced?*
>
> _____
>
> _____
>
> _____
>
> _____
>
> _____

In John 8:59, we read about the Jewish crowds in Jerusalem: "So they picked up stones to throw at Him, but Jesus hid Himself and went out of the temple."

But God protected Jesus just as He had protected David. In fact, David had two chances to slay Saul, but he refused both times, instead entrusting himself to God's care and keeping. Eventually, King Saul was mortally wounded in battle, and he killed himself by falling on his own sword.

2 Samuel

We do not know who wrote 2 Samuel; it was likely a successor of Samuel. The events in 2 Samuel followed the death of Saul and surrounded David, the ancestor of Jesus Christ who took the throne and ruled over Israel as God desired.

❀ DAVID ASCENDS TO THE THRONE ❀ AGAINST A RIVAL

After Saul's death, the people of the tribe of Judah made David their king, while Saul's son Ish-bosheth declared himself king. After a brief civil war, Ish-bosheth was murdered and David was declared king over all Israel.

⤙ Read 2 Samuel 5:1–5.

> *What did the people mean when they said, "When Saul was king over us, it was you who led out and brought in Israel" (v. 2)?*

One reason Saul had become so jealous of David was the people's recognition that David—not Saul—deserved credit for Israel's victories (see 1 Samuel 18:7).

As king, David fought many battles for Israel, freeing his people from all the enemies on every side that had plagued them during the time of the judges. He brought peace to their land.

The first thing he did was capture Jerusalem. Then he brought the ark of the covenant up into the city.

⤙ Read 2 Samuel 6:12–15.

> *Of what event in Jesus' life might this entrance of the ark into Jerusalem remind us?*

The ark was the symbol of God's presence among His people, and in Jesus Christ, God was dwelling among His people bodily. In both David bringing the ark of the covenant up into Jerusalem and Jesus entering Jerusalem in triumph, God Himself was entering Jerusalem, and His people were receiving Him with great praise and rejoicing.

After a time, David thought it was time for God's ark of the covenant to stop dwelling in a tent. David set out to build the Lord a glorious temple instead.

✤ GOD WOULD BUILD DAVID A HOUSE ✤

⤙ Read 2 Samuel 7:4–17.

> *What is so important about this prophecy?*

The line of the promised Messiah ran from Eve through Abraham, Isaac, and Jacob. It ran on through Rahab and Ruth and would now lead through King David to the Messiah; this is why the crowds in Jesus' day often called Him the "Son of David."

❈ CONCLUSION ❈

By God's grace, Israel reached the high point of its Old Testament history. David was the king against whom all other kings would be measured. And his line would lead to the promised Messiah and Savior, Jesus Christ. Next time, we will complete our look at the Historical Books of the Old Testament as we move ever closer to the coming of Jesus Christ.

❈ CLOSING PRAYER ❈

Lord Jesus Christ, You brought Your people into the Promised Land and forgave them when they strayed from You to worship foreign gods. Forgive us for the times we turn away from You, and set our hearts again to fear, love, and trust in You alone, our Savior, Deliverer, and King. Amen.

SESSION 4

❊ OPENING PRAYER ❊

Lord God, heavenly Father, the people of Israel put their faith in sinful human kings, who often led them astray. Thank You for raising up prophets to warn Your people and each of us. Thank You also for protecting Your people when they were exiled for their sinful rebellion, and for bringing them back home again. Remind us that in Jesus Christ, You have forgiven all our sins. Guide us by Your Word until that Last Day, when You will send Your Son to raise us all to life eternal and bring us into Your presence forever. In Jesus' name. Amen.

❊ INTRODUCTION ❊

In the last session, we saw God bring Israel into the Promised Land by His servant Joshua. We noted the spiritual decline after Joshua's death, during the period of the judges. Then we traced the first two kings over Israel, Saul and David. Today we take an in-depth look at Israel's split into two kingdoms, their fall, and how God still preserved the line and the promise leading to Jesus Christ.

1 Kings

The Books of 1 and 2 Kings were written by anonymous Israelite scribes. The events in these books took place after the reign of David, tracing the history of Israel's two kingdoms until both were exiled. The Book of 1 Kings begins with the reign of David's son Solomon, then recounts the split of the kingdom during the reign of Solomon's son. Unquestionably, the high point of 1 Kings is Solomon building the temple his father, David, had intended to build.

❊ SOLOMON BUILDS THE TEMPLE ❊

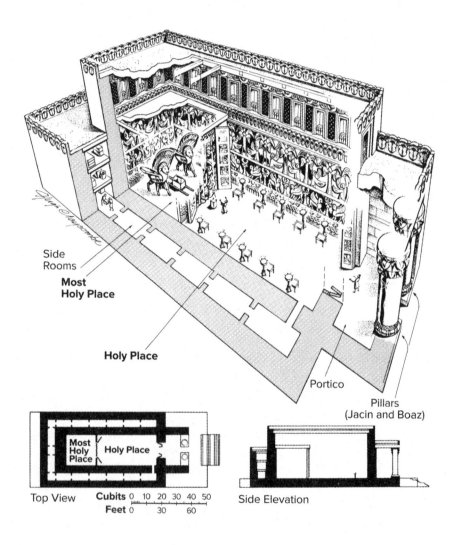

Side Rooms

Most Holy Place

Holy Place

Portico

Pillars (Jacin and Boaz)

Top View — Most Holy Place — Holy Place

Cubits 0 10 20 30 40 50
Feet 0 30 60

Side Elevation

◦ Read 1 Kings 8:1–11.

> *What was so significant about the temple?*
>
> ....
>
> ....
>
> ....
>
> ....
>
> ....

Until this time, the ark of God's presence had dwelt in the tabernacle, the movable tent Moses had constructed on Mount Sinai. Finally Solomon brought the ark of the covenant into a permanent place. The temple was the permanent place of sacrifice in Israel, the symbol of God's presence among His people—an object that foreshadowed Jesus dwelling among God's people in His human body. Though this temple would be destroyed because of Israel's unfaithfulness, it would be rebuilt, as recounted in the Book of Ezra. Within the courts of this rebuilt temple, Jesus would one day stand to teach the people when He was in Jerusalem. The destruction and rebuilding of the temple also foreshadowed the death and resurrection of Jesus Christ.

God blessed King Solomon with great wisdom and wealth, but in the years after he built the temple, Solomon disobeyed God's commands that He had given through Moses and married many, many foreign women in an attempt to secure peace with neighboring nations. He built palaces for these wives and temples and places of worship for their foreign gods. This led Solomon and Israel into idolatry. As punishment, God announced to Solomon that during the reign of his son, ten tribes would be yanked away from the line of David. David's sons would rule only the small Southern Kingdom of Judah, while other kings would rule the northern ten tribes, called Israel.

In 1 Kings, we see that the Southern Kingdom of Judah had a few notable, praiseworthy kings who followed in the footsteps of their ancestor David and served God faithfully. But in the Northern Kingdom of Israel, every single king was evil and worshiped false gods. The worst of them was King Ahab and his detestable foreign wife, Jezebel. Yet even in these darkest times in Israel, God raised up two of the greatest Old Testament prophets: Elijah and Elisha. The first of these had an interesting connection to the life of Jesus.

❈ ELIJAH THE PROPHET ❈

↝ Read 1 Kings 17:1–7.

> *How did Elijah point to Jesus?*
>
> ....
> ....
> ....
> ....
> ....
> ....

Actually, Elijah foreshadowed Jesus' forerunner, John the Baptist, more than he foreshadowed Jesus (Luke 1:17). Like John, Elijah suddenly arose, carried on his powerful ministry, and abruptly disappeared. In many ways, when we look at Elijah, we see a glimpse of John. The biggest difference is that John the Baptist performed no miracles, whereas Elijah performed some great ones, including raising the dead. In that way, his ministry foreshadowed Jesus' far greater ministry. During Jesus' earthly life, Elijah appeared with Moses on the Mount of Transfiguration (Matthew 17:3).

2 Kings

Like 1 Kings, 2 Kings was most likely written by anonymous Israelite scribes. The events in this book occurred during the later kingdom years of the nations of Israel and Judah. During this time, God was faithfully moving the line of David closer and closer to the birth of the Savior while preserving the good news of the Savior's coming. The Book of 2 Kings covers the history of Israel, beginning with the transition from Elijah's ministry to Elisha's. Then it catches the downward spiral of the Northern Kingdom until it is conquered and exiled by Assyria. It goes on to discuss the downfall of the Southern Kingdom, Judah, and it ends with the Southern Kingdom being conquered and exiled in Babylon. We begin our study with Elijah and King Ahab in the Northern Kingdom of Israel.

❀ ELIJAH TAKEN UP TO HEAVEN ❀

During Ahab's reign, God accomplished great things through Elijah. But eventually the time came when Elijah's work was finished. As he prepared to hand over his mantle to Elisha, Elijah was led from place to place, retracing the steps of Israel as they entered the Promised Land under Joshua. Finally, God sent chariots and horses of fire and a great whirlwind to carry Elijah up to heaven.

⤙ Read 2 Kings 2:6–14.

> *How did Elijah's manner of leaving the earth foreshadow Jesus' departure?*

❀ ELISHA'S MIRACLES ❀

Following Elijah's departure, God worked many great miracles through His prophet Elisha.

⤙ Read 2 Kings 5:1–14.

> *How did Elisha's miracles foreshadow Jesus?*

Working through Elisha, God healed Naaman of leprosy (2 Kings 5:10–14), raised to life a child who had died (4:32–37), and restored to life a man whose dead body was thrown on top of Elisha's corpse (13:20–21). But Jesus performed far more numerous and greater miracles than Elijah and Elisha did. Jesus healed large numbers of people with leprosy, blindness, deafness, and the inability to walk or to speak. He drove out demons, stilled storms, walked on water, fed huge multitudes with just a little bread and a few fish, and raised at least three people from the dead.

THE PLOT AGAINST THE SAVIOR'S LINE

All the kings of the Northern Kingdom of Israel were wicked unbelievers. But among David's descendants in Judah there were many good kings. One was Jehoshaphat. He was a believer, but he foolishly sought an alliance with ungodly King Ahab of Israel. He married his son, Jehoram, to a daughter of Ahab named Athaliah. Their son Ahaziah took the throne after his father's death. When Ahaziah was murdered by Israel's new king Jehu, who had assassinated all of Ahab's family at God's command, Athaliah claimed the throne of Judah. She set out to destroy all her grandchildren so she would be sole ruler, and in the process she threatened to extinguish the entire line leading to Jesus.

Read 2 Kings 11:1–3.

How did God save Ahaziah's youngest son, Joash, and keep the line leading to Jesus intact?

....

....

....

....

Jehosheba, Joash's aunt, was married to the priest Jehoiada. Jehoiada faithfully hid this ancestor of Jesus in the temple until he was eight years old. Then, taking two divisions of Levites who were temple guards, Jehoiada proclaimed Joash king, and when Athaliah came to see what was happening, the Levites separated her from her supporters, dragged her out of the temple, and put her to death. Joash was placed on the throne of David in Jerusalem.

In the remaining chapters of 2 Kings, we see the promise of the Savior passed from generation to generation.

❈ THE FALL OF ISRAEL ❈

Up in the Northern Kingdom of Israel, things continued to degenerate. After the death of King Ahab, no king of Israel ever quite reached his level of evil, but none that followed him sought to serve the Lord either. Despite the warnings of many prophets, which we will see in session 8, the ten tribes that made up the Northern Kingdom of Israel never returned to the Lord in repentance. Finally, in 732 BC, God brought in the Assyrian Empire to destroy Israel's capital of Samaria and take the Israelites into captivity. The Northern Kingdom never returned and was lost to history. They are sometimes called "the ten lost tribes of Israel."

In that time, Assyria also invaded the Southern Kingdom of Judah, capturing every fortified city and surrounding and laying siege to the capital, Jerusalem. When God heard the prayers of faithful King Hezekiah, He brought salvation to Jerusalem.

❧ Read 2 Kings 19:15–21, 32–36.

> *How did God save Jerusalem?*
>
> _____
>
> _____
>
> _____

To save us from Satan's power, God sent one man, His Son, Jesus Christ, who died in our place and gave us victory over all our enemies.

Hezekiah was a faithful, believing king, as was his great-grandson Josiah. But his other descendants were ungodly. Turning to foreign gods, they brought destruction upon themselves and upon Jerusalem.

❈ THE FALL(S) OF JERUSALEM ❈

In 597 BC, Jerusalem was captured by the Babylonians. Its king, Jehoiachin, was taken captive, along with the princes, the nobility, and those who were educated or were skilled craftsmen. These included Ezekiel the priest, and Daniel and his three friends—Shadrach, Meshach, and Abednego. The Babylonian king, Nebuchadnezzar, was unwilling to destroy the temple at that time. He put Jehoiachin in prison and appointed his uncle as a puppet king.

But over the next ten years, Judah's new king rebelled against Nebuchadnezzar. Then, in 587 BC, after a long siege, Jerusalem fell a second time. This time, Nebuchadnezzar took all but the poorest people into exile, looted the temple and burned it to the ground, and tore down the walls surrounding Jerusalem.

❈ KING JEHOIACHIN RELEASED FROM PRISON ❈

With Judah exiled in Babylon, it looked as though God's plan of rescue by the promised Savior had died. But God was at work among the exiles, preserving His people, His promises, and the line leading to the Savior. Near the end of 2 Kings, we read of a miraculous rescue God made.

⤚ Read 2 Kings 25:27–30.

Why was the release of King Jehoiachin important?

If Jehoiachin had remained in prison, there is a good chance he never would have had an heir, and the line from Eve through Abraham, Isaac, Jacob, and King David would have been cut off. But God arranged for his release instead. Jehoiachin spent the rest of his days in security, dining in a favored place at the Babylonian king's table. Jehoiachin's grandson Zerubbabel was the governor the king of Persia sent to rebuild Jerusalem and the temple when he permitted the exiled Jews to return to Jerusalem.

1 Chronicles

Both 1 and 2 Chronicles were most likely written by the priest and scribe Ezra. The books cover the same historical ground as all the previous historical books from Genesis through 2 Kings. But they do much of this through genealogical lists—lists of the people who lived during each of those time periods.

The books of 1 and 2 Chronicles were written to Jewish exiles who had been permitted to return to rebuild Judah and Jerusalem (we'll see their story in Ezra and Nehemiah). These exiles faced great difficulties. The land was covered with mounds of rubbish, remains of the devastation the Babylonians left behind. Even worse, they were surrounded by enemies who ridiculed, threatened, and opposed them in every way they could, including sending inflammatory letters to the Assyrian emperor, protesting their efforts to rebuild the temple and Jerusalem.

The books of 1 and 2 Chronicles were written to encourage these exiles to remember God's faithfulness despite the unfaithfulness His people had shown throughout the past. God had protected them through their exile, and He brought them back to rebuild. They could trust God's promises for them, especially His promise to send the Messiah. The Book of 1 Chronicles covers the period of time from Adam and Eve to King David, while 2 Chronicles recounts the time from King Solomon to the people's return from exile.

At first glance, it might seem difficult to find any reference to Jesus and His life through the long lists of genealogies that begin 1 Chronicles. But one of the most important genealogies is the line of people leading from Adam and Eve through Abraham, Isaac, Jacob, and David to Jesus Himself. Each of those names represents a lifetime lived on earth—family, friends, work, and play. Most are little more than names to us, but each was known to God and precious to Him, just as you and I are. Two incidents that fall toward the end of 1 Chronicles give us a glimpse into Jesus' life.

❀ DAVID BRINGS THE ARK INTO JERUSALEM ❀

In 1 Chronicles 11, the chronicler described how David captured the city of Jerusalem from the Jebusites, the Canaanite inhabitants of the land. He made it his own stronghold, and he prepared to bring the ark of the covenant into his city. This recollection of David rebuilding the shattered city of Jerusalem would encourage the returned exiles, since they were doing the same thing David had done before.

❧ Read 1 Chronicles 15:25–28.

> *What connection might there be between David bringing the ark into Jerusalem and events in the life of Jesus?*

Just as David had the ark brought into Jerusalem with great rejoicing and celebration, Jesus' final entry into Jerusalem on Palm Sunday was accompanied by great celebration and rejoicing, from Jesus' disciples and from the large crowds of Jews who were there to celebrate the Passover.

❀ DAVID'S CENSUS BRINGS PESTILENCE ❀

❧ Read 1 Chronicles 21:1–4, 7–27.
Twice, God commanded Moses to take a census of Israel, but David's census was against God's will. A light was shone on Jesus' suffering and death in this event.

> *How did this event foreshadow the sacrifice of Christ?*

In verse 17, David was pleading with God to stop punishing the people for his sin and punish him and his father's house instead. It would be David's descendant Jesus who would bear that punishment on the cross to spare all people from God's wrath. Furthermore, the spot on which David built the altar was the place where Solomon would build the temple. Nearby was the place where Jesus would sacrifice Himself to end the pestilence of death and hell we all deserve for our sinful disobedience against God.

As 1 Chronicles closes, David was anticipating his son Solomon building the temple. He amassed huge stocks and resources from which Solomon could draw the necessary materials to build the temple. He even received the design from God and passed it down to his son. The Book of 1 Chronicles ends with David organizing and establishing the priests and Levites in anticipation of them leading Israel's worship at the new temple—God's permanent dwelling place among His people. That new temple would likewise be a symbol of Jesus Christ, in whom God permanently dwells among His people.

2 Chronicles

The events in 2 Chronicles extend from the reign of David's son Solomon to the end of the Babylonian exile, when the Jews returned to Jerusalem to rebuild the temple. The Book of 2 Chronicles shows God's faithfulness to His people by keeping the line leading to Christ intact despite the dangers of exile due to the faithlessness of Israel.

The Book of 2 Chronicles begins with new King Solomon worshiping at the tabernacle in Gibeon.[2] At the tabernacle, Solomon prayed for wisdom and discernment. Then he made plans to build the temple.

---

2   The ark had been separated from the tabernacle, or tent of meeting, ever since the high priest Eli's sons removed it in 1 Samuel 4:4. At that time, it was captured by the Philistines; then it was returned to Israel without ever being placed back inside the tabernacle. David brought the ark into Jerusalem in 1 Chronicles 15, but he left the tabernacle in Gibeon.

❃ THE ARK IS BROUGHT INTO THE TEMPLE ❃

Solomon built the temple of the Lord according to the design plans his father, David, had given him (1 Chronicles 28:11–19). He assembled all the leaders of Israel in Jerusalem, and the Levites carried up the ark, the tent of meeting, and all its furnishings, uniting them once again inside the temple. Music was provided by the priests and Levites whom David had organized to lead the temple worship (1 Chronicles 25).

⬩ Read 2 Chronicles 5:2–14.

> *According to the chronicler, at what moment did the cloud of the Lord's glory fill the temple?*

The chronicler was reminding the returned exiles that when they rebuilt the temple, God would fill it in the same way.

The Book of 2 Chronicles records Solomon's reign, choosing not to mention his many foreign wives and his idolatry in building temples and places of worship for their foreign gods. When the chronicler described the split of the twelve tribes into two kingdoms, he focused on tracing the Southern Kingdom of Judah and the descendants of David who led to the promised Savior.

Many of the kings who descended from David were decent kings with faith, but they were not fully committed to serving God, as their father David had been. A classic case is King Jehoshaphat. He allied himself with the most wicked king of the Northern Kingdom of Israel, King Ahab. His alliance went so deep that he participated in an arranged marriage between his son Jehoram, who would reign after him, and a daughter of King Ahab, Athaliah. As we learned during our study of 2 Kings, this union almost proved disastrous for the messianic line when Athaliah's husband and son died and she seized the throne of Judah.

At that time, Jehoiada the priest organized the leaders of Judah with the Levite guards to proclaim Joash king, and Athaliah was executed. As king, Joash was faithful in his youth. But after Jehoiada died (at the ripe old age of 130), Joash abandoned the Lord and even turned against Jehoiada's faithful son, whom God sent to call him back to repentance.

❖ Read 2 Chronicles 24:20–25.

> *What is so ironic about what Joash did to Zechariah, Jehoiada's son?*

Interestingly, this brings up a judgment Jesus uttered against the Jewish leaders on Tuesday of Holy Week. In Matthew 23, Jesus unleashed a fiery witness against the Pharisees in Jerusalem, and He closed with a reference to the stoning of Zechariah.

❖ Read Matthew 23:29–36.

> *Why did Jesus include Zechariah with Abel here?*

It is striking that when Jesus was crucified by the workings of the Jewish religious leaders, He cried out, "Father, forgive them, for they know not what they do" (Luke 23:34). Likewise, when Stephen was being stoned, he prayed, "Lord, do not hold this sin against them" (Acts 7:60).

Concerning this judgment of Jesus, it is interesting to note that in the Hebrew Bible, the books are in a different order. The last book of the

Old Testament is Chronicles. Therefore, in the Hebrew Bible of Jesus' time, just four chapters into the first book, Genesis, Abel is murdered. And the twelfth-last chapter of the final book has Zechariah's stoning. Jesus was referring to each and every believer who was put to death by unbelievers throughout the entire Old Testament.

Three kings followed Joash who did right in the Lord's eyes, yet they were not fully faithful to God. Then came King Ahaz.

❀ FAITHLESS KING AHAZ ❀

⤳ Read 2 Chronicles 28:1–6, 10–27.

> *What did such a faithless man like Ahaz have to do with Jesus?*

Far more important, it was to wicked King Ahaz that the prophet Isaiah announced the great prophecy of the virgin birth of the Christ (Isaiah 7:1–2, 10–14).

Ahaz's son turned out to be one of the greatest kings of Israel, like David.

❀ HEZEKIAH CLEANSES THE TEMPLE ❀

⤳ Read 2 Chronicles 29:3–11, 15–19.

Hezekiah must have been horrified by the unfaithfulness of his father, Ahaz, who closed the temple and filled it with all kinds of filth and idolatry. Hezekiah's first act as king was to restore the temple and right worship in Israel.

> *Of what event in Jesus' life does this cleansing of the temple remind us?*
>
> _____
>
> _____
>
> _____
>
> _____
>
> _____

Sadly, all the good Hezekiah did was undone by his son Manasseh, who turned out to be the most wicked king from the line of David. The list of his sins is frightening: he rebuilt the high places of Ahaz; he built altars to false gods and set up their images in the temple; and he burned his sons as offerings to false gods. Yet his story has a surprising ending.

❈ MANASSEH'S REPENTANCE ❈

➤ Read 2 Chronicles 33:10–16.

Manasseh's repentance surely could not atone for the grievous sins he had committed, especially the murder of his sons. But his descendant Jesus Christ would pay the price for Manasseh's sins—and yours and mine—when He laid down His life on the cross.

The Book of 2 Chronicles quickly moves to Manasseh's grandson, Josiah, a righteous king on the level of Hezekiah and King David. He restored worship at the temple and even cleansed the false gods from the territory of the northern kings of Israel, which by this time had been conquered by Assyria. Sadly, Josiah died when he foolishly went out to fight the king of Egypt against God's word of warning (2 Chronicles 35:20–24).

After Josiah's death, Judah quickly declined. Three of Josiah's sons and one of his grandsons reigned, but each was evil and was quickly disposed of by Egypt and then Babylon. Finally, Jerusalem was captured by Babylon and its people were exiled.

But 2 Chronicles ends on a positive note after Judah had been in exile seventy years.

❈ THE PROCLAMATION OF CYRUS ❈

❧ Read 2 Chronicles 36:22–23.

How did this passage point to Jesus Christ?

....

....

....

....

Ezra

◇◇◇◇◇◇◇◇◇◇◇◇◇◇◇

Ezra was a Jewish priest who became the first scribe, or expert in "the Law," that is, the books of Scripture. He wrote this book and likely 1 and 2 Chronicles as well. The events in this book occurred near the end of the Old Testament era as God brought His people back from the Babylonian exile to rebuild the temple in Jerusalem in preparation of Jesus' birth. Ezra described the first two waves of Jews returning from exile in Babylon.

In chapters 1–6, Ezra told how these exiles rebuilt the temple under the leader of the tribe of Judah, who was named Zerubbabel. (He was a descendant of Jehoiachin, the exiled king of Judah who was in the line leading to Christ [Matthew 1:12–16].) This was a significant event, particularly because the Northern Kingdom of Israel never returned from its captivity. Those ten tribes were lost, absorbed into the surrounding nations. The same thing easily could have happened to Judah. But God faithfully preserved them and brought them back.

In fact, this captivity and restoration was similar to Israel's four hundred years of slavery in Egypt. The family of Jacob easily could have disappeared into the Egyptian nation, but God preserved it, and by His mighty arm, brought Israel out of their Egyptian captivity to freedom in the Promised Land.

The line of David remained intact, and one of David's descendants, Zerubbabel, was the governor who led the first group of exiles to return and begin rebuilding the temple. In the temple courts Zerubbabel built, our Lord Jesus would one day stand and teach the crowds about the kingdom of heaven.

❊ GOD STIRS HIS PEOPLE ❊ TO RETURN TO JERUSALEM

❖ Read Ezra 1:2–7.

By this time, Persia had conquered Babylon. Notice that God stirred not only the Gentile emperor Cyrus to issue his proclamation. He also stirred up the Jewish family leaders (elders) and the priests and Levites to leave their exilic homes and return to rebuild the ruins of Jerusalem and the temple.

Ezra 2 includes a detailed list of the returning exiles. This explains why many Bible scholars believe Ezra was the chronicler who wrote 1 and 2 Chronicles.

❊ THE EXILES REBUILD THE ALTAR ❊

❖ Read Ezra 3:1–6.

> *Why did the Jews rebuild the altar before they began rebuilding the temple?*

How might this relate to Jesus Christ? When Jesus cleansed the temple in John 2, the Jewish religious leaders demanded a miraculous sign showing His authority to do this. Jesus answered, "Destroy this temple, and in three days I will raise it up" (John 2:19). Jesus compared the destruction of Solomon's temple and its rebuilding by the returned exiles to His death and resurrection. It is interesting that before rebuilding the temple, they rebuilt the altar of sacrifice. And before the resurrection of Jesus' body came the altar of the cross on which His body was "destroyed."

❈ REBUILDING THE TEMPLE ❈

The rebuilding of Solomon's temple foreshadows Jesus' resurrection.

↝ Read Ezra 4:1–6.

These adversaries would come to be known as the Samaritans. They were exiles from various countries who had been brought into the land of the Northern Kingdom by the Assyrians when the ten tribes were exiled. (For a more complete picture of their background, read 2 Kings 17:24–41.) The fact that these people were predominantly Gentiles with false religions contributed to the hostility between Jews and Samaritans in Jesus' day. But their opposition to the rebuilding of the temple and walls of Jerusalem (described in Nehemiah) made this hatred even stronger. This helps to explain how shocking it was when Jesus befriended the Samaritans and even used one of them as the hero in His parable of the Good Samaritan (Luke 10:25–37).

❈ FACING OPPOSITION ❈

The returned exiles faced great opposition from their Samaritan neighbors. This included threats, discouragement, bribes for counselors against them, and official accusations against the Jews to the Persian king. One of these kings halted construction.

↝ Read Ezra 4:17–24.

> *Why did King Artaxerxes decide to halt construction on the temple?*

Persian King Artaxerxes did not wish to lose this territory. Throughout history, kings of Judah had rebelled against Babylonian kings. Some of the sons of Josiah, for instance, had broken their covenant with Babylon to ally themselves with the Egyptians. Artaxerxes feared they would rebel against Persia, too, so he halted the construction in an effort to exercise control over the city and thwart the possibility that an uprising might happen again.

But verse 24 offers a glimmer of hope: "until the second year of the reign of Darius king of Persia."

❀ CONSTRUCTION RESUMES ❀

Construction halted until Artaxerxes was succeeded by Darius. Then, inspired by the prophets Haggai and Zechariah, Zerubbabel led the returned exiles to resume construction. When the Persian governor over that province questioned them, he took down their names and consulted with the king, but he permitted construction to continue in the meantime.

King Darius received the letter and ordered a search of the archived documents. That search resulted in finding Cyrus's original decree. Based on this decree, Darius published his ruling.

➻ Read Ezra 6:6–12.

> *How were Tattenai, the Persian governor, and Darius, the Persian king, crucial to the completion of the temple?*

Ezra recorded the completion of the temple and the first celebration of the Passover in the newly rebuilt structure, proof that God had not abandoned His people during the exile or rescinded His covenant with them. That Passover reminds us of the Passover to come when Jesus would die on the cross to save us from the angel of death.

❀ EZRA IS SENT ❀

More than five decades passed between the completion of the temple and the arrival of Ezra the priest. During that time, the crucial events recorded in the Book of Esther took place.

Over those five decades, the temple became neglected, Levites left their service at the temple, and the people neglected the Lord. God moved the Persian king to send Ezra and give him the authority to reform worship practices in Jerusalem.

-⋆ Read Ezra 7:25–26.

> *What authority did the king give to Ezra?*

Through Ezra the priest, God restored proper worship, arranged for the support of the Levites, and brought the people back in repentance.

Nehemiah

The events in the Book of Nehemiah began about twelve years after the events in the end of Ezra. Nehemiah was a Jew who served as the cupbearer to the Persian emperor Artaxerxes. Artaxerxes's father, Ahasuerus, was the king who took Esther as his queen.

The cupbearer was a very trusted position. He was the king's last line of defense against poisoning—a very common method for assassinating ancient kings. This would be very important when Samaritan enemies threatened to tell the king that Nehemiah was raising a rebellion against him. Nehemiah knew that Artaxerxes would realize it was all a lie.

Nehemiah's mission in Jerusalem began when he talked with some Jews from Jerusalem who had come to the capital.

-⋆ Read Nehemiah 1:1–11.

Though the temple had been rebuilt, it was a dangerous time in Jerusalem. The city walls were lying in ruins and the inhabitants were exposed to raids from the Samaritans and other enemies.

> *What promises of God did Nehemiah claim in his prayer?*

Jesus gave us wonderful promises and even gave us words to pray to our heavenly Father in the Lord's Prayer. By God's grace, Nehemiah sought and received authority from the king to go to Jerusalem to rebuild the city walls.

When he arrived in Jerusalem, Nehemiah went out by night to inspect the city walls (Nehemiah 2), then announced his plans and lined up workers, who began construction on the wall (chapter 3).

❀ NEHEMIAH AROUSES THE JEALOUSY ❀ OF HIS ENEMIES

↝ Read Nehemiah 4:1–9.

> *Which people opposed Nehemiah's work for Jerusalem and for God?*

Sanballat and the Samaritans first used ridicule and mockery to intimidate the workers. When that failed and he learned that the work on the wall was progressing rapidly, he and his people plotted to go and fight against Jerusalem. These would have been secretive, guerrilla-style attacks, since the king's letters commanded local officials to cooperate with Nehemiah.

Jesus was familiar with such tactics from His own enemies. He faced accusations and rumors, threats and intimidation (Luke 13:31–33) before His enemies resorted to an illegal night trial and railroaded Pilate into crucifying Him.

Like Jesus, Nehemiah put his trust in God and faithfully did his work, completing the wall around Jerusalem. The Book of Nehemiah closes with further reforms he enacted with the help of Ezra the priest.

Esther

The events in the Book of Esther took place in the decades between Zerubbabel rebuilding the temple and Ezra's arrival in Jerusalem, followed by Nehemiah's work of restoring the walls of Jerusalem.

Esther was a beautiful Jewish orphan raised by her cousin Mordecai in exile. She was chosen to be the queen of Persia after King Ahasuerus banished his first wife.

Esther describes the ascension of an evil man, Haman, who was an adviser to the king. He was lifted up above all of the king's other officials and became prime minister over Persia. But he was proud and arrogant. The king ordered all people to bow down to Haman, and when Haman saw Mordecai refusing to bow, he became extremely enraged. But instead of merely seeking Mordecai's death, Haman plotted to convince Ahasuerus to order the extermination of all of Mordecai's people, the Jews.

⭗ Read Esther 3:12–15.

What was so dangerous about this plot?

One odd thing about the Book of Esther is that it never directly mentions God by name. But it could only be God who could foil Haman's plot and save His people as He had promised.

When Mordecai read the edict, he sent word to Esther and begged her to intercede with the king on behalf of her people.

❀ MORDECAI CALLS ON ESTHER ❀ TO SAVE THE JEWS

❧ Read Esther 4:8–17.

> *What did Mordecai mean when he said, "Relief and deliverance will rise for the Jews from another place" (v. 14)?*

Esther appealed to her husband the king, and when he truly came to understand Haman's plot, his anger burned. He ordered Haman's execution, and he gave Mordecai authority to protect the Jews by allowing them to assemble to defend themselves against their enemies.

The Persian king Ahasuerus provides an unlikely comparison to Jesus Christ in the Book of Esther. Like the king, Jesus is captivated by His Bride, the Church. When she is in danger, His anger is greatly kindled, and no foe can stand against Him.

❀ CONCLUSION ❀

This session followed the line of David as it progressed from generation to generation, ever closer to the birth of God's Son, our Savior, Jesus Christ. Despite the faithless kings and people of Israel, God was faithful to His covenant promise. He preserved His people and even brought them back from captivity, always keeping the family line leading to the Savior intact.

The Old Testament history of Israel closes some four hundred years before Christ's birth. Jerusalem had been reestablished, the temple was rebuilt, and worship had been restored. The only thing remaining before Christ's birth was for God to prepare the world's political scene. Persia must give way to Alexander the Great and Macedonia, and the Macedonians must fall to the Romans. All of this tumult occurred in the four centuries before Christ's birth, and all of it was prophesied in Daniel 10 and 11.

Next we turn to the Poetic Books, which reveal the life, death, and resurrection of Jesus Christ in amazing and unexpected detail.

❀ CLOSING PRAYER ❀

Lord God, heavenly Father, thank You for sending prophets to Your wayward people, calling them to repentance and faith; and then, when the kings and people refused, protecting them through their exile and finally bringing them back to rebuild the temple in preparation for the birth, life, and ministry of Your Son, Jesus Christ. Guide Your people in faith through this life, and protect us from all harm. For Jesus' sake we pray. Amen.

SESSION 5

Lord Jesus Christ, thank You for the gifts of poetry, music, and art. Thank You especially for inspiring the writers of the Wisdom Literature, who reveal Your glory and tap into our deepest sorrows, fears, joys, hopes, adoration, and praise. Send Your Spirit to guide us as we seek You in the Bible's Wisdom Literature. Amen.

Christ in the Wisdom Literature

In this session, we turn from the Historical Books to the next five books of the Old Testament, the Wisdom Literature: Job, Psalms, Proverbs, Ecclesiastes, and Song of Solomon. These books were written as Hebrew poetry. They teach us how to live out our faith, resist the temptations of our sinful nature, and show God's love in the midst of a fallen, broken world. Since God sent His Son to share our life in this broken world and to suffer and die for our sins, it should not be surprising to see the promise of God's Son appear over and over in the Bible's Wisdom Literature.

Job

Why does God let bad things happen to the people who trust in His promise of salvation through His Son, our Lord Jesus Christ? The Book of Job explores the suffering and heartache believers face in this sin-stained world. It teaches us to humble ourselves and trust God when we cannot understand how and why He permits suffering and evil to afflict us.

We do not know the author of Job, though Job might have written it. We also do not know the date of its writing. Job may well have lived in the days of Abraham, Isaac, and Jacob. Job was a believer who was wealthy, influential, and much respected by his neighbors. As we learn in chapter 29, he feared God, protected and provided for those around him who were in need, and rose up to stop evildoers from taking advantage of his neighbors.

⤳ Read Job 29:11–25.

> *How would you describe Job's position before troubles befell him?*

Job was not perfect, but as a forgiven believer in God's promise of salvation through the coming Savior, he modeled a wonderful life. He used his social position and the wealth God had given him to greatly improve the lives of those around him.

Life was good for Job until the day God mentioned his uprightness to Satan.

⤳ Read Job 1:6–22.

We may wonder why God pointed out the uprightness of Job's faith to Satan. But Satan's answer shows his complete inability to understand what faith is. He was convinced Job had no real love for God—that Job served God only so he would continue to enjoy his wealth and privilege. To teach Satan that faith does not depend on our material success, God permitted him to take away all Job's possessions and kill his precious children.

In a single day, Job lost everything—his wealth and his seven sons and three daughters. Yet Job's response was an expression of pure faith:

Naked I came from my mother's womb, and naked shall I return. The LORD gave, and the LORD has taken away; blessed be the name of the LORD. (JOB 1:21)

> *How do you think Job was able to answer in faith rather than in hurt and anger?*

The next day (Job 2), God pointed out how Job had lost everything, yet he still blessed God. Satan viciously accused Job of selfishly praising God because in all the carnage, Job himself had not been personally harmed. This again betrays Satan's total selfishness, and that of our sinful nature. He had no genuine love or concern for the angels he led into rebellion against God. And he was no true friend to Adam and Eve—or to any sinner he tempts. Satan made the false accusation that the only person who mattered to Job was Job himself. What a horrible, insensitive claim to make against Job, who, of course, was deeply grieved by the death of each of his ten children.

God granted Satan permission to test his theory on Job. He afflicted Job with disease and covered him in sores. Job sat in pain, grief, and misery, scratching his itchy skin with broken pottery. Yet even with this, Job refused to curse God—even when his wife urged him to do so.

✦ Read Job 2:9–10.

Who were the "foolish women" Job mentioned to his wife?

Job still clung to his trust in God:

Shall we receive good from God, and shall we not receive evil? (JOB 2:10)

Job had three friends. When they heard of the great loss Job had suffered, they came together to comfort him. Their resulting discussion with Job fills most of the book as they struggle to explain why suffering falls upon believers in this life.

❀ JUDGING BY APPEARANCES ❀

Job's friends believed they could tell how God felt about someone by considering the circumstances of that person's life. They reasoned that God rewarded the righteous and punished evildoers. So those people who were healthy and prosperous and had a good reputation were righteous. But if they were sickly, poor, and despised, God was punishing them for a specific sin.

To Job's friends, his sufferings and loss were clear proof that the righteous God was punishing him for some great evil he had committed and had tried unsuccessfully to hide. At first, Job's friends gently called on him to repent and confess his sin. When he kept refusing to do so, they pressed harder and harder and became more direct and severe in their accusations against him.

✦ Read Job 4:7–11.

> *What indirect accusation did Eliphaz make?*

It is so easy for people who are at ease and free of suffering to judge and condemn those who are suffering, and to assume that suffering and loss are evidence of a sin or a failing.

But Job teaches us that we cannot judge any person's relationship with God based on circumstances in that person's life—not even our own life. Otherwise, it is easy to think God is punishing us for a sin He already forgave or that God is cruel and evil, as Job nearly concluded.

Actually, this same kind of judgment happened to Jesus. Right up to the time they found Him hanging on the cross, the crowds in Jerusalem believed He might possibly be the promised Messiah, David's greater Son. As with Job, everyone spoke well of Jesus—until they saw Him flogged, beaten, and crucified. Then the crowd's estimation of Jesus changed drastically.

And those who passed by derided Him, wagging their heads and saying, "Aha! You who would destroy the temple and rebuild it in three days, save Yourself, and come down from the cross!" (MARK 15:29–30)

That word "Aha" expresses their feeling that God had used Jesus' sufferings to expose Him as a fraud and a fake. Paul mentioned how this false perception made it difficult to preach Jesus to the Jews:

But we preach Christ crucified, a stumbling block to Jews and folly to Gentiles. (1 CORINTHIANS 1:23)

❈ THERE IS NO MEDIATOR ❈

Job saw it differently than his friends did. Like them, he believed God punished evildoers and rewarded the faithful and righteous.

But knowing he had not committed any great sin to deserve such suffering, he struggled to understand why God was being unfaithful to him, since God knew that Job trusted Him and befriended others.

But even though Job knew he was not guilty of a great unrepented sin, he also knew he was just flesh, a lowly creature. He could not force God to see his point of view. He longed for someone to stand as a mediator or arbiter between himself and God—someone who would understand his point of view and speak with God on his behalf.

⤏ Read Job 9:1–12, 32–35.

Job was a mere mortal, in absolutely no position to stand before God and demand justice. He knew God was the almighty Creator of the heavens and the earth. Job would need someone equal to God to be able to mediate on his behalf.

> *How does this passage point to Jesus Christ?*
>
> ....
>
> ....
>
> ....
>
> ....

Job was suffering desperately—physical agony on top of the grief of losing all ten of his children. He realized his insignificance in comparison with God. Though he believed in God's love and grace, he needed a mediator, a man who could reason with God and bring peace. Jesus is that man: the God-man who brought peace and reconciliation between God and sinful humans by His perfect life of obedience and by His innocent suffering and death on the cross in our place.

Of course, Jesus is not only our mediator with God. He is also the sacrifice who took our guilt, sin, and sufferings upon Himself when He died on the cross. Job also brilliantly prophesied and found comfort in Jesus' resurrection.

❈ I KNOW THAT MY REDEEMER LIVES ❈

⤏ Read Job 19:21–27.

What is remarkable about this prophecy?

In his time of deepest suffering, Job found comfort in God's promise to send the Savior to bruise the serpent's head. He found comfort in the death and resurrection of that Mediator and Savior God had promised to Adam and Eve in Genesis 3.

Finally, in chapters 38–41, God Himself appeared to Job to remind him that mere mortals cannot understand His works and His ways, so we must live by faith and trust in His mercy and grace for the sake of the promised Savior, Jesus Christ.

At the end of Job, God restored Job's health, property, and possessions, and He gave him and his wife ten more children: seven sons and three daughters. From the vantage point of this life, God restored Job's ten children. But in the wider eternal reality, Job knew that God had given him twenty children—ten who were with him on earth, and ten more who were waiting for him after death. Through this, God gave us a glimpse into our blessed future in the new heavens and the new earth because of Jesus Christ, our Savior.

Psalms

Psalms is the hymnbook for Israel, a collection of songs and prayers written under the Holy Spirit's inspiration over a number of centuries by various authors, including Moses, David, Solomon, and Levites who directed worship at the temple.

Most of the psalms were written by David. As 1 Chronicles clearly shows, King David was instrumental in establishing Israel's worship. Being a gifted musician and writer, and full of the Holy Spirit, he was uniquely gifted to accomplish this.

⟿ Read 1 Samuel 16:14–23.

> *How might this experience have influenced David's thoughts about Israel's worship?*
>
> _____
>
> _____
>
> _____
>
> _____
>
> _____

David not only wrote and composed many psalms and their musical accompaniment, but he also organized the Levites, assigning musicians and Levitical choirs. Indeed, when his son Solomon dedicated the temple in 2 Chronicles 5, all the Levitical singers were dressed in fine linen, and they accompanied the proceedings with cymbals, harps, and lyres. With them were 120 priests with their trumpets. When they raised their voices and instruments to praise the Lord, the house of the Lord was filled with the cloud of God's glorious presence.

Likewise, every time we gather to worship and raise our voices in praise of our God, the glory of the Lord enters our midst, as Jesus promised: "For where two or three are gathered in My name, there am I among them" (Matthew 18:20).

The Psalms cover every emotional experience we face in life, from joy and worship to fear, sorrow, guilt, and loneliness. In God's Son, Jesus, our sins are forgiven and we are given access to pray to God in any and every situation and circumstance in life.

At least eight psalms speak directly of the life of Christ (2, 22, 24, 45, 61, 72, 110, and 118). We will look at a few psalms that point directly to events in Jesus' life.

❈ JUDAS'S BETRAYAL ❈

⟿ Read Psalm 41.

David wrote about an incident that occurred when his son Absalom rose up against him and attempted to seize his throne (see 2 Samuel

15–18). Absalom was assisted by David's trusted counselor, Ahithophel, who betrayed David and joined Absalom's rebellion. Ahithophel guided Absalom to sever all ties with David and persuade the people that David's rule was ended. If Absalom had followed his counsel, his troops likely would have killed David and his rebellion would have succeeded. But God caused Absalom's plot to fail when he took the advice of a different counselor, Hushai. Hushai pretended to be loyal to Absalom, but he was actually still faithful to David. When Absalom followed Hushai's advice, David escaped, and Ahithophel knew David would regroup his men and defeat Absalom's army in battle. Foreseeing Absalom's defeat, Ahithophel went home, put his house in order, and hanged himself (2 Samuel 17:23).

How is this similar to Judas's betrayal of Jesus?

The similarities between David's experience and Jesus' experience at the Last Supper are striking. Judas ate at Jesus' table and even received bread from Jesus' hand. Later, Judas, who had agreed to betray Jesus for thirty pieces of silver, led Jesus' enemies to the Garden of Gethsemane. There he greeted Jesus and kissed Him so the guards would know precisely whom to seize.

After Judas saw that Jesus was condemned, he was filled with remorse. He returned the silver coins to the chief priests and confessed his sins. When they refused to have anything to do with him, Judas threw the silver pieces into the temple, then went out and hanged himself. The similarity to Ahithophel's betrayal of David and later hanging himself is truly quite eerie.

❀ JESUS' CRUCIFIXION, DEATH, ❀ AND RESURRECTION

↝ Read Psalm 22.

David wrote this haunting psalm about one thousand years before Jesus' crucifixion, yet it includes stunning details about the sufferings of our Lord on Good Friday.

First, the opening words are the exact same words our Lord uttered from the cross, piercing the darkness in the ninth hour:

"My God, My God, why have You forsaken Me?"
(MATTHEW 27:46)

When we look closely at the following verses in this psalm, they very powerfully describe Jesus' agony as He hung from the cross.

- "I am a worm and not a man" (Psalm 22:6). People who were crucified suffered constant agony. They twisted and writhed in a vain effort to find a comfortable position that alleviated their suffering.
- "All who see me mock me" (Psalm 22:7). David even writes the very words that were spoken against Jesus by the crowds and the chief priests: "He trusts in the LORD; let Him deliver him; let Him rescue him, for He delights in him!" (Psalm 22:8). Now compare these words with Matthew 27:43: "He trusts in God; let God deliver Him now, if He desires Him. For He said, 'I am the Son of God.'"
- "All my bones are out of joint" (Psalm 22:14). The weight of Jesus' body hanging from His hands would have made all His joints feel like they were being pulled apart. His only relief would have been when He tried to stand, pushing against the nails in His feet.
- "My tongue sticks to my jaws" (Psalm 22:15). Jesus expressed this when He cried, "I thirst" (John 19:28).

- "They have pierced my hands and feet" (Psalm 22:16). Oddly enough, none of the crucifixion accounts in the Gospels speak specifically of the soldiers nailing Jesus to the cross. But Jesus' resurrection appearance to Thomas in John 20 makes it clear that Jesus was nailed to the cross:

The other disciples told him, "We have seen the Lord." But he said to them, "Unless I see in His hands the mark of the nails, and place my finger into the mark of the nails, and place my hand into His side, I will never believe." (JOHN 20:25)

- "They divide my garments among them, and for my clothing they cast lots" (Psalm 22:18). The soldiers divided Jesus' clothing into four piles, then cast lots for His long, seamless tunic (John 19:24).

In Psalm 22, King David related intricate descriptions of Jesus' crucifixion (vv. 1–20), but he also prophesied Jesus' resurrection and the results it would bring (vv. 21–31). This psalm reads as if Jesus were speaking to us directly from the cross and the empty tomb. It is not a coincidence that Jesus spoke the first line of this psalm as He was hanging on the cross (Matthew 27:46).

❈ JESUS' ASCENSION ❈

✦ Read Psalm 110.
Jesus quoted this psalm on Tuesday of Holy Week, completely silencing the challenges from the scribes, Pharisees, and Sadducees, "If then David calls Him Lord, how is He his son?" (Matthew 22:45; see also Mark 12:37 and Luke 20:44).

How can Jesus be both David's Lord and David's son?

This psalm also gives us a glimpse into the heavenly perspective of Jesus' ascension on the fortieth day after His resurrection. He ascended through the clouds, passed in victory through the host of heaven, and took His place at the right hand of God the Father.

Proverbs

◇◇◇◇◇◇◇◇◇◇◇◇◇◇◇◇◇◇◇◇◇◇◇◇◇◇◇◇◇◇◇

The next three books of the Bible—Proverbs, Ecclesiastes, and Song of Solomon—were all written by King David's son Solomon, except for the latter chapters of Proverbs. Most Bible scholars are convinced Solomon wrote Song of Solomon in his youth, Proverbs in his middle years, and Ecclesiastes late in his life.

Solomon was famous for his wisdom. Early in his reign, he made a great sacrifice to God, and that same night, God appeared to him in a dream and told him to request what he wanted. Solomon could have asked for riches, long life, or the death of his enemies. Instead he asked for discretion to know right from wrong so that he would be able to lead God's people Israel. God was very pleased and gave him what he requested, a wise and discerning heart (1 Kings 3). The Book of Proverbs reveals this wisdom.

Solomon wrote the majority of the proverbs in the book, though he did compile some wise sayings by other wise people. Basically, the proverbs in this book contrast the wisdom of living in faith toward God with the folly of rejecting God and living without Him. Proverbs fills an important role in our Christian life. It provides wise guidance for living our lives as children of God through faith in Jesus Christ.

In that way, it is very similar to Jesus' Sermon on the Mount in Matthew 5–7, in which Jesus began with Gospel promises, then taught His followers how they could live under God's righteous rule.

Jesus is not directly mentioned in Proverbs. But when Solomon personifies Wisdom as a lady calling and instructing young people, we see a close parallel to Jesus in His teaching ministry.

❀ WISDOM CRIES ALOUD IN THE STREETS ❀

↝ Read Proverbs 1:20–33.

> *How might this passage remind us of Jesus' public ministry?*

This passage could really serve as a commentary on Jesus' teaching ministry throughout Galilee and in Jerusalem. He went to "the lost sheep of the house of Israel" (Matthew 15:24), who were convinced they could please God by their works and taught them about sin and righteousness, God's undeserved mercy, and His free gift of faith and salvation.

❀ WISDOM AND CREATION ❀

Proverbs speaks much about wisdom, even going beyond the earlier discussion of how to live our lives as children of God. In Proverbs 8, Solomon spoke about the place of wisdom as God created the world. In this poetic description, it is very easy to see Jesus sitting at His Father's side, working with Him to create everything. This makes it a perfect companion piece to the first verses of the Gospel of John.

↝ Read Proverbs 8:22–36.

> *Why is it important to remember Jesus' role in creating the world?*

Jesus' work in creation explains His great love for His human creatures. He has a personal investment in every human because He made us all. He loves us so much that He became human and lived among us. Through His perfect obedience, innocent suffering and death, and glorious resurrection, He has power to save us from sin, death, and hell, and the authority to judge and punish all those who reject Him. It is wonderful to see how He rejoices in all the creatures that live in His inhabited world, and how He delights in mankind.

Ecclesiastes

Bible scholars believe that Solomon gathered his proverbs in his middle years and wrote our next book, Ecclesiastes, in his old age. It is a book written for people of all ages—but it seems as if Solomon was speaking especially to warn the young people who see their lives open before them and this whole wide world inviting them to indulge in all the pleasures it has to offer. In Proverbs, he let Wisdom instruct the young to warn them against the trap of sin. In Ecclesiastes, he spoke from his own miserable experiences.

Solomon was the perfect one to write this book. With his great wealth and power, he allowed himself to freely indulge his desires in all that this world has to offer. He spoke from experience after having misused the wisdom and wealth God gave him by disobeying God's commands, marrying hundreds of foreign women who led him into idol worship, and seeking the rewards of pleasure and its pursuit.

It can be difficult to find Jesus in the Book of Ecclesiastes. Like Proverbs, the book was written to teach people how to live—but unlike Proverbs, it teaches about the emptiness, vanity, and meaninglessness of a life that has been lived apart from God. Jesus is not mentioned directly, but His teachings carry similar themes to those Solomon recorded in this book, especially about life without God.

❈ SATISFYING OUR DESIRES ❈

❧ Read Ecclesiastes 2:24–26.

Solomon counsels us to live in simple gratitude to God for the daily bread He provides us.

> *How does the advice of Solomon fit with Jesus' parable of the rich fool in Luke 12:16–21?*

God tells us that rather than focusing all our attention and placing all our hopes on satisfying our sinful desires, or working tirelessly for our future goals and plans, He wants us to enjoy the simple day-to-day blessings He gives us, trusting Him to provide for our future and satisfy our desires with good things.

❈ WHILE WE LIVE, THERE IS TIME TO REPENT ❈

❧ Read Ecclesiastes 9:4–5.

Solomon reminds us that *today* is the day to repent, while we still have access to God's grace through the promised Savior.

> *What is the danger of waiting to repent until later in our life?*

That repentance is especially important when we focus on the plans and goals we have set for our lives—milestones we wish to reach because we think they will give our lives meaning and fill us with contentment and joy. We can so easily build up these milestones in our minds to the point that they become false gods upon which we place our hope for all the comfort, joy, and meaning we anticipate in our lives. They can easily overshadow our daily enjoyment of the work God has given us and all the wonderful blessings He gives us each day.

But most important, these earthly dreams and goals can come to preoccupy our attention, turning our minds from our need for God's forgiveness and the salvation Jesus won for us. They can distract us from the far greater and more meaningful things God wants to share with us through all eternity. If we cast aside repentance and faith while straining to achieve the earthly goals we set for ourselves, we can easily find ourselves at the end of life with no time left to repent.

❊ OUR LAST DAYS ❊

✎ Read Ecclesiastes 12:11–14.
In powerful poetic language, Solomon depicted the weakness, pain, and suffering old age brings upon people.

> *What event involving Jesus did Solomon speak of here?*
>
> _____
>
> _____
>
> _____
>
> _____

Ecclesiastes warns of the emptiness of life in this world and urges God's people to find purpose and meaning in a life of simple faith, which God has graciously provided for Jesus' sake. Even if it does not directly speak to God's promise of salvation in Jesus Christ, this Wisdom Literature reminds us that in our promised Savior, God has good purposes for our life and wants us to find value in our life here on earth—and much more so with Him in heaven.

Song of Solomon

This book is also known as Song of Songs. This means that of all the 1,005 songs he wrote (1 Kings 4:32), Solomon considered this to be his greatest.

Though the Song of Solomon describes the courtship, betrothal, and marriage of Solomon and his bride the Shunammite, it has a wider application to Jesus Christ, the Groom, and His Bride, the Church.

In Israelite culture, both in Old Testament and New Testament times, marriages were arranged by parents, often when the future bride and groom were still children. When the couple were old enough, they became betrothed in a ceremony that made them officially and legally husband and wife. Yet, throughout the time of betrothal, which usually lasted from nine months to a year, the husband and wife lived apart, while the husband prepared a home for his wife. Then, when all things were ready, the groom returned for his bride and brought her to the wedding feast, where their life together began.

Two passages in Song of Solomon apply particularly well to Jesus Christ.

❀ THE HEAVENLY WEDDING BANQUET ❀

Jesus used betrothal language when He sat with His disciples in the Upper Room on the night in which He was betrayed. He said:

> **In My Father's house are many rooms. If it were not so, would I have told you that I go to prepare a place for you? And if I go and prepare a place for you, I will come again and will take you to Myself, that where I am you may be also.** (JOHN 14:2–3)

The time in which we are living falls between Jesus' ascension and His return on the Last Day to judge the living and the dead. This is called the New Testament period, and we can think of it as our betrothal period. Our Groom, Jesus Christ, has gone to prepare a heavenly home for us, and when the Father's set time has come, He will return with all

His angels to take us to Himself. Jesus often described that wonderful day in parables, referring to it as a wedding banquet.

❧ Read Song of Solomon 2:3–4.

> *What does the phrase "His banner over me was love" mean?*

Christ's banner is His great love by which He defends His Church in this world, protects us from our enemies (the devil, the world, and our own sinful nature), and makes all things work together for our good.

❈ LOVE IS STRONG AS DEATH ❈

Christ's love for His Bride moved Him to become human, come to this earth, and live among us. It caused Him to go to the cross to save His Bride and purify her of her sins. That love is clearly shown in the next passage.

❧ Read Song of Solomon 8:6–7.

> *What does it mean to say, "Love is strong as death" (v. 6)?*

This passage reminds us of Romans 8:35–39, "Who shall separate us from the love of Christ? . . ." God's Son went through death to win His Bride, and He triumphed over death when He rose to life, victorious over it, on the third day.

We believers are the Bride of Christ. As you read Song of Solomon, may God deepen your yearning for Christ's return and the life He will give us eternally with Him in heaven.

❀ CONCLUSION ❀

In the Wisdom Literature, God provides us a glimpse into His loving heart, and He invites us to bring all our worries, fears, and doubts to Him. In Jesus Christ, He forgives us and fills us with the hope of everlasting life. The Holy Spirit works through these books to sanctify our lives, that we may live in the fear and love of God, awaiting with joy the day of our Savior's glorious return and our eternal life with Him.

❀ CLOSING PRAYER ❀

Lord God, heavenly Father, we thank You for sharing Your divine wisdom with us in the Holy Scriptures. Fill us with Your Holy Spirit and the wisdom from above, that we may cling to Jesus, our Savior, through life and death, and share His great story of salvation wherever we are. In Jesus' name we pray. Amen.

SESSION 6

❁ **OPENING PRAYER** ❁

Lord Jesus Christ, throughout the Old Testament, You spoke to the prophets, and through them to Your people Israel. Thank You for the special books written by these servants, for they show us our sin and foretell Your great work of salvation through Your Son, Jesus Christ. Guide us by Your Spirit that we may find Your salvation and all its comfort, joy, and hope in their words. Amen.

The Prophetic Books

In this session, we begin the third and final section of the Old Testament, the seventeen Books of the Prophets. Today we look at three writings from the first two so-called "major prophets." They are called major prophets because of the length of their writings, not because these prophets themselves were more important than the so-called "minor prophets" who follow them.

Isaiah

Isaiah was not the first prophet God raised up for Israel. Moses was a prophet, as was Samuel, the last of the judges. During David's reign, God raised up the prophet Nathan. And as we discussed with regard to 1 Kings, God raised up Elijah and Elisha as prophets in the time of King Ahab.

The difference between those prophets and these later prophets is that the writings of these prophets were gathered together into individual books, whereas the words of the earlier prophets were recorded within the Historical Books, as we have already seen.

Isaiah was a court prophet whose ministry occurred about seven hundred years before the birth of Jesus Christ. Isaiah had access to the royal court of the kings of Judah. Of all the books of the Old Testament, Isaiah reveals the most to us about Jesus' life and work.

Isaiah begins with God's promise to wash away the sin of His people.

⊷ Read Isaiah 1:15–18.

> *What kinds of sins would have turned the hands of the Israelites scarlet and crimson?*

It is reassuring to hear that even vicious sins like murder can be washed away by the blood of the Savior promised to Adam and Eve, Jesus Christ.

❀ BORN OF A VIRGIN ❀

Isaiah's first prophecy about Jesus came at a time of great danger in Judah. The mighty and savage Assyrian Empire was pressing on Israel and Syria, Judah's neighbors to the north. These small nations were trying to build an alliance against the Assyrians, and they were pressuring and threatening Judah's unfaithful King Ahaz to unite with them. God promised Ahaz that those two nations would fall but that He would faithfully defend Judah. God even offered to give a sign to reassure Ahaz and give him confidence in God's deliverance.

⤳ Read Isaiah 7:10–14.

> *How was this prophecy of Christ's virgin birth a sign to Ahaz?*

By expanding on the promise of the coming Savior, God was giving Ahaz the chance to anchor his confidence and trust in God's deliverance. Ahaz easily could have found peace and hope by trusting in the promises of his God, but he refused to accept God's offer or put his trust in the promised Savior.

In the first chapter of the Gospel of Matthew, Joseph learned that his betrothed wife, Mary, was pregnant. When he considered divorcing her, an angel told him her child, Jesus, was from the Holy Spirit. Matthew then used this prophecy from Isaiah to teach that Mary was pregnant with the Son of God by the power of the Holy Spirit.

> But as he considered these things, behold, an angel of the Lord appeared to him in a dream, saying, "Joseph, son of David, do not fear to take Mary as your wife, for that which is conceived in her is from the Holy Spirit. She will bear a son, and you shall call His name Jesus, for He will save His people from their sins." All this took place to fulfill what the Lord had spoken by the prophet: "Behold, the virgin shall conceive and bear a son, and they shall call His name Immanuel" (which means "God with us"). When Joseph woke from sleep, he did as the angel of the Lord

commanded him: he took his wife, but knew her not until she had given birth to a son. And he called His name Jesus. (MATTHEW 1:20–25)

Ahaz rejected this promise, but for us who believe, Jesus' conception and birth of a virgin guarantees that our Savior was not contaminated by the sinful nature we inherited from our sinful parents. He is a pure and holy Sacrifice, able to save us from God's eternal wrath by His innocent suffering and death.

❋ FOR TO US A CHILD IS BORN ❋

After this prophecy, Assyria swept south, conquering Syria and Israel. They exiled the Israelites, scattering them throughout their territory so that the ten tribes were lost. Assyria swept on southward, invading Judah and capturing every fortified city. They laid siege to Jerusalem and easily would have conquered Judah, but God sent an angel who killed a large number of Assyrian soldiers, forcing them to flee back to the north (see Isaiah 36–37). With the northern tribes of Israel gone, Isaiah gave another prophecy about the birth of the Savior. It began with the land once occupied by the tribes of Zebulun and Naphtali in Israel, and it promised that the Messiah would preach in that northern area, which is called Galilee in the New Testament.

➤ Read Isaiah 9:1–7.

> *Why does this prophecy mention "the throne of David" (v. 7)?*

The words of this prophecy are glorious, showing the increase of Jesus' kingdom, which we witness today and all throughout the New Testament era as more and more people are brought to faith through the Word and Sacraments.

❈ I WILL PUT MY SPIRIT UPON HIM ❈

Isaiah gave another prophecy that was fulfilled when Jesus was anointed by the Holy Spirit, following His Baptism by John the Baptist at the age of thirty.

↝ Read Isaiah 11:1–10.

> *Why is Jesus described as a shoot coming forth from the stump of Jesse?*

Old Testament prophets often described kingdoms as massive trees (see Ezekiel 31:3; Amos 2:9). Isaiah used this metaphor to describe the kingdom of David. Jesse was the father of David and thus ancestor to all of Judah's kings. When the Babylonians conquered Jerusalem, the reign of David's sons was ended—and in that figure of speech the tree was cut down and only a stump remained for centuries. Then, when David's Son Christ was born, it was as if a shoot of life came forth from that dead stump—a shoot that would become the mighty tree, far surpassing David.

Another important feature of this prophecy is the Spirit of the Lord resting on Jesus. This prophecy was fulfilled when the Spirit came down on Jesus in bodily form as a dove after He was baptized. The Spirit alighted on Jesus and remained on Him. That was the moment Jesus was anointed by God, set apart as the *Christ*, the *Messiah*, which are the Greek and Hebrew words for "the Anointed One" (see Matthew 3:16).

❈ GOD WILL SWALLOW UP DEATH ❈

After a series of chapters in which Isaiah pronounced God's judgment against the nations surrounding Israel and then against Israel itself, Isaiah prophesied the judgment of the whole earth in Isaiah 24, a prophecy of Judgment Day when Jesus Christ will return to judge the living and the dead. That led to a stirring prophecy of the victory over death that the Christ would win by His death and resurrection and the victory over death He would bring to earth at His second coming.

❧ Read Isaiah 25:6–9.

What mountain was Isaiah speaking of where God would make "a feast of rich food" for all peoples?

❈ A V O I C E C R I E S ❈

After more chapters on judgment and four historical chapters from the life of King Hezekiah, the tone of the book changes. It becomes more Gospel-centered, as the life and work of Jesus Christ is prophesied.

❧ Read Isaiah 40:1–5.

Of what person does this prophecy speak?

The Gospel of John records John the Baptist's use of this passage from Isaiah.

And this is the testimony of John, when the Jews sent priests and Levites from Jerusalem to ask him, "Who are you?" He confessed, and did not deny, but confessed, "I am not the Christ." And they asked him, "What then? Are you Elijah?" He said, "I am not." "Are you the Prophet?" And he answered, "No." So they said to him, "Who are you? We need to give an answer to those who sent us. What do you say about yourself?" He said, "I am the voice of one crying out in the wilderness, 'Make straight the way of the Lord,' as the prophet Isaiah said." (JOHN 1:19–23)

John was Jesus' great forerunner, and he brought great comfort to the people of Israel with the assurance that God's Messiah had come and God had raised up John to be His messenger to prepare His way and to reveal Him to Israel.

❁ BEHOLD, MY SERVANT ❁

Isaiah 42 provides a glimpse into Jesus' public ministry and how He would conduct it. Matthew cites verses 1–4 of Isaiah's words in Matthew 12:18–21.

↝ Read Isaiah 42:1–9.

Which action in Isaiah's prophecy grasps you the most?

In the verses of Matthew 12 immediately preceding the quotation from Isaiah 42 (Matthew 12:15–16), Jesus healed all who were sick and directed those who had been healed not to tell anyone what He had done. This is what Isaiah meant by Jesus not crying out for attention. Throughout His ministry, Jesus showed great patience and gentleness, carefully binding up the brokenhearted and fanning the flames of faith in those who were discouraged and fearful.

❊ CHRIST'S DEATH AND RESURRECTION ❊

In one of the most amazing passages in the Old Testament, Isaiah foretold the sacrifice of the coming Christ, explaining how He would save us from our sins.

❧ Read Isaiah 52:13–53:9.

> *On what aspect of Jesus' sacrifice did Isaiah center this prophecy?*
>
> _____
>
> _____
>
> _____
>
> _____
>
> _____

One of the greatest obstacles the apostles faced in sharing the story of Jesus' salvation with Jews was the stumbling block of the cross. It was a stumbling block because Jews firmly believed that God rewarded the righteous and punished the wicked. So when they saw a man honored and prosperous, they took it as evidence that he was a righteous man being rewarded by God. But if they saw a man suffering shame and dishonor, that was proof for them that he was a sinner being punished by God. God gave us the Book of Job to dispel this falsehood, and Isaiah likewise addressed it in 53:4: "Yet we esteemed Him stricken, smitten by God, and afflicted." Isaiah cuts to the heart of the Jewish objection against Jesus' crucifixion. The Jews reasoned that God would never punish an innocent man—let alone His own Son, the promised Messiah—with anything as severe and humiliating as crucifixion. So they took Jesus' crucifixion as clear evidence that God had unmasked Jesus of Nazareth as a fake and fraud.

But Isaiah made their misunderstanding clear. He surrounded that phrase with substitutionary terms that made clear the great exchange Christ made with us on that cross: "Surely He has borne our griefs and carried our sorrows. . . . But He was pierced for our transgressions; He was crushed for our iniquities" (Isaiah 53:4a, 5a). Any Jew who carefully analyzed Isaiah's prophecy would see the Holy Spirit remove the stumbling block of Jesus' crucifixion.

❧ Read Isaiah 53:10–12.

> *What words in this passage prophesy Jesus' resurrection?*

Isaiah's amazing prophecies of the life, work, death, and resurrection of Jesus Christ make this one of the most amazing books of the Old Testament. They provided groundwork that evangelists like Matthew would use to prove that Jesus of Nazareth is the Son of God and Savior of the world.

Jeremiah

Jeremiah prophesied about a century after Isaiah. His ministry ran through the declining years of the kingdom of Judah. He called on David's sons in the Southern Kingdom to repent of their sins, but his cries were ignored. He witnessed the invasion of Judah by Babylon. Until the fall of Jerusalem, his message could be nothing but Law, condemning the unrepentant people who refused to listen. His powerful words of doom and judgment sound like Jesus' judgment on the Pharisees and experts in the law in Matthew 23.

Jeremiah warned Judah's last king, Zedekiah, not to break his treaty with the Babylonians, but the king refused to listen to him. The prophet watched the Babylonian armies return and lay siege to Jerusalem. He watched the city's defenses fall and the Jewish captives being dragged off into the exile.

But once Jerusalem fell, when the vast majority had been either killed or exiled and the temple had been reduced to a smoldering pile of rubble, Jeremiah turned to proclaim God's mercy and forgiveness in the coming Messiah, Jesus Christ. Jeremiah himself was treated well because he had warned Zedekiah to keep his treaty with the Babylonians. He was given the choice to remain with the few inhabitants permitted to stay in Jerusalem or to go along with the exiles, where he would be treated well. Jeremiah chose to remain in the ruins of Jerusalem to minister to the survivors.

❀ JEREMIAH WEEPS FOR HIS PEOPLE ❀

When you thumb through the first eight chapters of Jeremiah, you find nothing but Law, judgment, threats, and condemnation. Finally, near the end of chapter 8, Jeremiah grieves for his people.

⟿ Read Jeremiah 8:18–9:1.

In the same way, in Luke 19:41–44, after entering Jerusalem, Jesus wept over Jerusalem's stubborn unbelief and the devastation that would come upon it "because you did not know the time of your visitation" (v. 44). The "visitation" was the coming of God's Son, the promised Savior. He lived among them. He spent three years teaching them, healing their sick, and casting out demons, but they did not believe in Him, nor did they turn from their sins in repentance and faith.

❀ THE RIGHTEOUS BRANCH ❀

⟿ Read Jeremiah 23:5–6.

> *Why is Jesus called a "Branch"?*
>
> _____
>
> _____
>
> _____
>
> _____
>
> _____
>
> _____

As the passage shows, Jesus is the righteous King who will "execute justice and righteousness," meaning He will rule in perfect holiness. And He would provide for His people to be righteous by taking their sins, their guilt, and their shame upon Himself and suffering God's wrath at our sins, while giving them and all of us believers His holiness to claim as our own by faith.

❀ THE CUP OF THE LORD'S WRATH ❀

Jeremiah hinted again at Jesus' sufferings in chapter 25, where he used the illustration of the cup of wrath. This powerful drink made those who swallow it stagger and stumble and collapse in a faint as though they were drunk. It vividly described the effects of God's punishment on the various nations and their kings who would suffer that wrath. Their cities would be encircled by enemy armies who would slowly starve them out. Then, when the people were weak, diseased, and staggering from hunger, the enemy would breach their walls and put them to the sword, captivity, and exile.

↝ Read Jeremiah 25:15–29. (If you can't pronounce the names of all the kingdoms in vv. 20–25, just skim through and count how many there are!)

> *How does this passage help us understand Jesus' prayer in the Garden of Gethsemane, "My Father, if it be possible, let this cup pass from Me; nevertheless, not as I will, but as You will" (Matthew 26:39)?*

Judah, Egypt, and all the nations mentioned in this passage suffered God's wrath for their sins, injustice, and idolatry when He brought in the armies of the Babylonian Empire to conquer them. In time, God punished the Babylonians for their cruelty by bringing in the Persian Empire to conquer *them.*

But despite all that these nations suffered, their suffering was not enough to satisfy God's wrath at their sins. Neither are the sufferings we endure throughout our earthly life, no matter how intense those sufferings may be. Only the suffering of God's perfect Son was able to satisfy God. Jesus Christ drank this cup of God's wrath down to the very dregs, adding new meaning to His proclamation from the cross "It is finished" (John 19:30). With the cup of God's wrath empty, Jesus now invites us to drink the cup of blessing, His precious blood poured out for us in Holy Communion.

❁ THIS MAN DESERVES DEATH ❁

God directed Jeremiah to go up to the temple courts and warn the people of Judah that if they refused to repent, God would desecrate and destroy the temple, leaving it completely desolate and abandoned.

❧ Read Jeremiah 26.

> *What does the phrase "like Shiloh" (vv. 6, 9) mean?*
>
> ....
>
> ....
>
> ....
>
> ....
>
> ....

When Israel conquered the Promised Land under Joshua's leadership, the city of Shiloh was the place where they erected the tabernacle with the ark of the covenant inside. This was the place where the Israelites would bring their sacrifices and gather for their feasts.

For about four hundred years throughout the time of the judges, Shiloh was the location where Israelites could seek God's presence. When the Israelites turned against God, He brought in the Philistines, who defeated Israel, captured the ark (1 Samuel 4–6), and completely destroyed Shiloh. The tabernacle was relocated to Gibeon (1 Chronicles

16:39), and when the ark was returned to Israel, it was kept in the house of Abinadab in Kiriath-jearim (1 Samuel 7:1–2). The ark remained there until David brought it up into Jerusalem. The tabernacle remained in Gibeon until Solomon built his temple and placed both the ark and tabernacle inside it. Shiloh was never rebuilt. It was a desolate ruin that stood as a somber warning to Israel that having the ark and the tabernacle in the temple would not automatically protect Solomon's temple and Jerusalem from destruction if Judah did not repent and believe.

The Israelites were furious when Jeremiah compared them to the people of Samuel's day, and they laid hold of him and tried to kill him.

> *How does the treatment of Jeremiah in this passage remind us of what Jesus suffered?*

At least Jeremiah was defended by faithful elders of Israel. No Israelites rose to Jesus' defense. Pontius Pilate, the Roman governor, tried to defend Jesus, but ultimately he handed our Lord over to the demands of the Jewish people to be crucified and killed.

❈ RACHEL WEEPING FOR HER CHILDREN ❈

In chapter 31, Jeremiah comforted Judah with the promise that God would restore the exiles to their land. Two New Testament events are connected with it. The first is Rachel weeping for her children.

⤷ Read Jeremiah 31:15–17.

> *Who was Rachel?*

Jacob had fled to his uncle Laban after stealing his brother Esau's blessing from his blind father, Isaac (Genesis 27). There he fell in love with Rachel, Laban's daughter, and he agreed to work for his uncle for seven years for the privilege of marrying her. After the seven years, Laban tricked Jacob and gave him his older daughter, Leah, in place of Rachel. With the promise of marrying Rachel, Jacob agreed to work for Laban another seven years. When Jacob had fathered eleven sons through his two wives and their servants, he brought his family back to Canaan. But along the way, Rachel died from complications of childbirth while she was giving birth to her second son. She named him *Ben-Oni*, meaning "son of my troubles," which is the reason Jeremiah speaks of her lamentation and bitter weeping. Mercifully, Jacob renamed him *Benjamin*, which means "son of my people" (Genesis 35:16–20). Rachel died in Ephrathah near the town that would be called Bethlehem, the future birthplace of King David and Jesus Christ.

Jeremiah turned the incident of Rachel's death around. The tribe of Rachel's son Benjamin had been absorbed by the tribe of Judah. Jeremiah was speaking of the tribe of Benjamin in this prophecy. Jeremiah described it as Rachel weeping for her children, the members of the tribe of Benjamin, who were there no more because they had been taken from their homes to live in exile in faraway Babylon.

In connection with what event in Jesus' childhood did Matthew use this passage?

Just as Rachel's dying tears and cries once echoed in this land at the birth of her child, the land of Bethlehem would once again be filled with bitter weeping and lamentation of the mothers when Herod's soldiers slew the little boys of Bethlehem in his vain attempt to murder Jesus.

Then Herod, when he saw that he had been tricked by the wise men, became furious, and he sent and killed all the male children in Bethlehem and in all that region who were two years old or under, according to the time that he had ascertained from the wise men. Then was fulfilled what was spoken by the prophet Jeremiah: "A voice was heard in Ramah, weeping and loud lamentation, Rachel weeping for her children; she refused to be comforted, because they are no more." (MATTHEW 2:16–18)

❋ THE NEW COVENANT ❋

Jeremiah spoke of a "new covenant," a new testament God would make with His people. A day was coming when God's people would no longer wander from Him but all would know Him.

◦ Read Jeremiah 31:31–34.

> *What was Jeremiah predicting in these words?*
>
> _____
> _____
> _____
> _____
> _____

When God poured out His Spirit on His apostles, it started a new era, one when the Holy Spirit would enter all believers in Baptism. Because of this, each of us can know God directly without the need for earthly priests and a high priest to serve as mediators between God and us. Now Jesus is that great High Priest and Mediator at the Father's right hand.

❋ A RIGHTEOUS BRANCH ❋

Jeremiah includes a wonderful prophecy about Jesus ruling Israel as David's son.

✧ Read Jeremiah 33:14–16.

What was Jeremiah teaching us about Jesus?

When we look at Judah's kings who were descended from David, we find that most of them were lacking. Few ruled in true justice and righteousness, and most led Judah into great sin and idolatry. But Jesus would not only lead Israel in justice; He also gives us peace and He *is* our righteousness.

Being sinners, we have no righteousness of our own. But by faith, Jesus has given us His own righteousness.

Lamentations

Jeremiah wrote the five chapters of Lamentations to express the sorrow, grief, and desolation in Jerusalem after it was laid waste by Babylon. This lament is an outpouring of grief and pain that can remind us of Jesus' sufferings on the cross.

❀ SHADOWS OF THE CROSS ❀

The first chapter of Lamentations compares Jerusalem to a childless widow, bereft of her husband and all her children. The city lay devastated and in ruins. Her anguish fit really well with Jesus' sufferings on the cross.

✧ Read Lamentations 1:12–14.

> *How does this passage apply to Jesus' crucifixion?*
>
> ....
>
> ....
>
> ....
>
> ....

Parts of this passage are used in the liturgy for Good Friday to portray the agony Jesus experienced as He paid the price for all of our sins on the cross. The words "from on high He sent fire; into My bones He made it descend" remind us of Jesus' great thirst. Though Jesus was innocent of any wrongdoing or sin, all of the sins of mankind, all our "transgressions were bound into a yoke; by [God the Father's] hand they were fastened together; they were set upon [Jesus'] neck" (v. 14).

❋ THE TEMPLE IS IN RUINS ❋

The greatest pride and joy of Jerusalem was the glorious temple Solomon had built. Now, because of Judah's sin, the temple had been demolished like a hut made of leaves and branches, the type of booths the people of Israel built for the Feast of Booths each year.

✤ Read Lamentations 2:6–7.

When Jesus cleansed the temple, He drove off the animals being sold in the temple courts and overturned the money-changers' tables. He told them, "Take these things away; do not make My Father's house a house of trade" (John 2:16). When the Jews objected, Jesus made a startling prophecy.

> So the Jews said to Him, "What sign do You show us for doing these things?" Jesus answered them, "Destroy this temple, and in three days I will raise it up." The Jews then said, "It has taken forty-six years to build this temple, and will You raise it up in three days?" But He was speaking about the temple of His body. When therefore He was raised from the dead, His disciples remembered that He had said this, and they believed the Scripture and the words that Jesus had spoken. (JOHN 2:18–22)

> *How can this passage remind us of Jesus' life?*
>
> ....
> ....
> ....
> ....
> ....
> ....

Jesus compared His death and resurrection to the destruction of the temple in Jerusalem by the Babylonian armies and its rebuilding seventy years later, when Persian King Cyrus permitted the exiles to return and rebuild the temple of the Lord.

❈ MY EYES FLOW WITH RIVERS OF TEARS ❈

In Jeremiah 3, the prophet confessed his sins and the sins of the people of Judah, and he announced God's just punishment for those sins. But he wept and grieved at the destruction of his people.

❧ Read Lamentations 3:46–51.

Jesus likewise shed tears when He foresaw the destruction of Jerusalem by the Romans.

> And when He drew near and saw the city, He wept over it, saying, "Would that you, even you, had known on this day the things that make for peace! But now they are hidden from your eyes. For the days will come upon you, when your enemies will set up a barricade around you and surround you and hem you in on every side and tear you down to the ground, you and your children within you. And they will not leave one stone upon another in you, because you did not know the time of your visitation." (LUKE 19:41–44)

What did Jesus mean by "the time of your visitation"?

In a similar way, the people of Jerusalem were guilty of the same during Jeremiah's day. God had visited them in the prophet Jeremiah and countless prophets like Isaiah before, who had warned them to repent and amend their sinful lives. But they had refused to believe. Their temple was looted and demolished; their city, burned and destroyed; and the vast majority of people, killed or exiled. How much worse would it be when the Jerusalem of Jesus' day refused to obey Him?

❈ CONCLUSION ❈

The prophets Isaiah and Jeremiah wrote amazing prophecies that unfolded much of the life, ministry, and work of Jesus Christ. They especially described His suffering, death, and resurrection and the amazing things He accomplished for all of us on the cross and through the empty tomb.

❈ CLOSING PRAYER ❈

Lord Jesus Christ, in Your prophets, You have given us a glimpse into Your great love and compassion that moved You to lay down Your life to save us. Kindle in our hearts a true joy and gratitude for Your loving sacrifice, that we may truly repent of our sins and put our faith in You throughout the days of our lives, that we may dwell with You throughout all eternity. Amen.

SESSION 7

❀ OPENING PRAYER ❀

Lord Jesus Christ, You raised up many prophets to call Your people to repentance and faith throughout the Old Testament, right up to its closing some four centuries before Your birth. Thank You for what You revealed to them about Your mission, which is recorded for us today as well. Guide us to see You clearly by Your Holy Spirit. Amen.

Ezekiel

◇◇◇◇◇◇◇◇◇◇◇◇◇◇◇◇◇◇◇◇◇◇◇◇◇

Ezekiel was a priest in Judah who was taken into captivity when Jerusalem first fell to the Babylonians in 597 BC. While Jeremiah remained in Jerusalem with the remnant there, God called Ezekiel to be a prophet to his fellow exiles.

God directed Ezekiel to confront a false hope to which the exiles were clinging. In God's great mercy, He had led the Babylonians to leave the temple standing in Jerusalem after they had taken the royal family of Judah, all the officials, and the educated and talented Jews to Babylon. Only the poor remained behind with Jeremiah. The sparing of the temple led the exiles to the false conclusion that God would soon bring them home, perhaps in a matter of months or, at most, a year or two.

Ezekiel confronted their delusions by exposing the grievous sins that were still going on at the temple, and by proclaiming God's furious wrath against those still living in the city. A day of judgment was coming soon for those who had remained in Jerusalem. The terrifying language of the Lord reminds us of Judgment Day—and the day two thousand years ago when God's judgment for all our sins fell on His Son hanging on the cross.

◦ Read Ezekiel 7:1–9.

How could this passage apply to Jesus, who is without sin?

This same thought was declared by John the Baptist shortly after he baptized Jesus.

> The next day he saw Jesus coming toward him, and said, "Behold, the Lamb of God, who takes away the sin of the world! This is He of whom I said, 'After me comes a man who ranks before me, because He was before me.' I myself did not know Him, but for this purpose I came baptizing with water, that He might be revealed to Israel." And John bore witness: "I saw the Spirit descend from heaven like a dove, and it remained on Him. I myself did not know Him, but He who sent me to baptize with water said to me, 'He on whom you see the Spirit descend and remain, this is He who baptizes with the Holy Spirit.' And I have seen and have borne witness that this is the Son of God." (JOHN 1:29–34)

As John mentioned, Jesus is the Lamb of God, the perfect sacrifice God had promised to provide as the substitute who would die in our place on the cross. Jesus Christ took onto Himself the fiery wrath of God the Father so that believers will not have to experience it on the Last Day.

❈ THE PRINCE TO WHOM JUDGMENT BELONGS ❈

Ezekiel spent most of the early chapters in his book convincing his fellow exiles that Jerusalem would be judged for its evil. In chapter 21, he returned to that theme. He spoke against Judah's last king, Zedekiah, whom he called a "prince," and foretold the end of his reign in Jerusalem.

◦ Read Ezekiel 21:24–27.

> *What did Ezekiel mean when he wrote, "A ruin, ruin, ruin I will make it," and, "This also shall not be" (v. 27)?*

Yet, at the end of this passage, Ezekiel predicted Jesus' coming in the words "until He comes, the one to whom judgment belongs, and I will give it to Him" (v. 27). That is why it is significant that the crowds who welcomed Jesus into Jerusalem on Palm Sunday, the first day of Holy Week, called Him the Son of David.

And many spread their cloaks on the road, and others spread leafy branches that they had cut from the fields. And those who went before and those who followed were shouting, "Hosanna! Blessed is He who comes in the name of the Lord! Blessed is the coming kingdom of our father David! Hosanna in the highest!" (MARK 11:8–10)

The title "Son of David" that was often used of Jesus was a confession that He was the Messiah, or Christ, God had promised to David in 2 Samuel 7:11–12.

❈ A HORN SHALL SPRING UP ❈

Zedekiah, the king of Judah, broke his treaty with Babylon after forming an alliance with Egypt. In chapters 29–32, Ezekiel spoke of the defeat of Egypt's armies at the hands of the Babylonians, a defeat that would open the door for the Babylonian armies to return and utterly destroy Jerusalem in 587 BC. But in one easily overlooked verse, God gave a very short messianic prophecy that pointed ahead to Jesus.

↝ Read Ezekiel 29:21.

What was the significance of a horn in the Old Testament?

After John the Baptist's birth, his father, Zechariah the priest, made a prophecy about Jesus, the Son in Mary's womb.

And his father Zechariah was filled with the Holy Spirit and prophesied, saying, "Blessed be the Lord God of Israel, for He has visited and redeemed His people and has raised up a horn of salvation for us in the house of His servant David, as He spoke by the mouth of His holy prophets from of old, that we should be saved from our enemies and from the hand of all who hate us; to show the mercy promised to our fathers and to remember His holy covenant, the oath that He swore to our father Abraham, to grant us that we, being delivered from the hand of our enemies, might serve Him without fear, in holiness and righteousness before Him all our days." (LUKE 1:67–75)

Jesus Christ is the mighty horn God the Father raised for us. He defeated Satan, sin, and hell in His death on the cross, and He crushed death under His feet when He rose to life on the third day.

Finally, in Ezekiel 33:21, the prophet received the report from a fugitive of Jerusalem that the city had fallen and the temple had been destroyed. For the exiles, it was a dark and hopeless time. But at this very point, Ezekiel's book turned from the powerful condemnation of the Law to the sweet Gospel promises of the Savior and the restoration He will bring.

❀ THE GOOD SHEPHERD ❀

One of the clearest places to see Jesus in the Book of Ezekiel is the chapter following the account of the exiles receiving news of Jerusalem's destruction. The temple had been looted and burned and was lying in ruins. With the temple lost, the exiles gave up all hope of ever returning to Canaan. They felt abandoned and cut off forever, a nation that would disappear, as the northern ten tribes had. That's when God gave Ezekiel a beautiful promise of the coming Savior to restore their hope.

↬ Read Ezekiel 34:11–16.

> *How did this comfort the exiles? How can it comfort us?*

Jesus picked up this language in His beautiful words from John 10.

I am the good shepherd. The good shepherd lays down His life for the sheep. He who is a hired hand and not a shepherd, who does not own the sheep, sees the wolf coming and leaves the sheep and flees, and the wolf snatches them and scatters them. He flees because he is a hired hand and cares nothing for the sheep. I am the good shepherd. I know My

**own and My own know Me, just as the Father knows Me
and I know the Father; and I lay down My life for the sheep.**
(JOHN 10:11–15)

We are also far from our home in the Garden of Eden and God's
presence—Christians who are scattered among all the nations of the
earth. Often we live in cultures that are hostile to Jesus Christ and His
message of salvation. Yet through Word and Sacrament, our Shepherd
seeks us out, gathers us into His flock, and guides us to our home in
heaven. When Christ returns to judge the world, He will gather us
all together from the ends of the earth. He will judge and remove all
unbelievers and restore His creation so we can live with Him forever
in the new heavens and the new earth.

❈ GOD WILL REUNITE ISRAEL ❈

Israel was a divided kingdom because of the idolatry of David's son
Solomon. During the reign of Solomon's son Rehoboam, God divided
the kingdom of Israel into two kingdoms. These two nations lived side
by side but usually in great hostility. In this prophecy, God promised
to remove the divisions between His people Israel forever.

↝ Read Ezekiel 37:21–28.

> *Who is God's "servant David," who would be king over His
> united people?*
>
> _____
>
> _____
>
> _____
>
> _____
>
> _____

Ever since Adam and Eve's fall in the Garden of Eden (Genesis 3),
the human race has been divided between believers and unbelievers.
And as we have seen, Christians are often divided from one another.
The night before Jesus died, He predicted His death to His disciples,

but He promised to rise again. He promised to come and dwell among us and make His home within us as He guides us to heaven.

> "I will not leave you as orphans; I will come to you. Yet a little while and the world will see Me no more, but you will see Me. Because I live, you also will live. In that day you will know that I am in My Father, and you in Me, and I in you. Whoever has My commandments and keeps them, he it is who loves Me. And he who loves Me will be loved by My Father, and I will love him and manifest Myself to him." Judas (not Iscariot) said to Him, "Lord, how is it that You will manifest Yourself to us, and not to the world?" Jesus answered him, "If anyone loves Me, he will keep My word, and My Father will love him, and We will come to him and make Our home with him. Whoever does not love Me does not keep My words. And the word that you hear is not Mine but the Father's who sent Me." (JOHN 14:18–24)

❈ EZEKIEL'S TEMPLE ❈

So much of the first half of the Book of Ezekiel revolves around the temple in Jerusalem, which was the center of the exiles' false hopes. The devastating destruction of the first temple was God's punishment on the sins of Israel, just as the destruction of Jesus' body on the cross was God's punishment for the sins of all people. But having completely satisfied His Father's wrath, the Savior did not stay dead in His grave, but rose to new, glorious, and eternal life.

Ezekiel concluded his book with the perfect vision of a new and glorious temple. He was representing the reign of the promised Messiah among His people. But the temple was the perfect picture for that reign. For the exiles stranded far from home, with no temple left in Jerusalem to pray toward, the best way for them to picture the glorious kingdom of the Messiah was through a new temple, which God would raise to replace the first.

⤙ Read Ezekiel 47:1–2.

> *What does the water flowing from the temple symbolize?*
>
> _____
>
> _____
>
> _____
>
> _____
>
> _____
>
> _____

John's Gospel picked up on this theme of water in several places. The first was when Jesus met a Samaritan woman by a well.

> **If you knew the gift of God, and who it is that is saying to you, "Give Me a drink," you would have asked Him, and He would have given you living water. . . . Everyone who drinks of this water will be thirsty again, but whoever drinks of the water that I will give him will never be thirsty again. The water that I will give him will become in him a spring of water welling up to eternal life.** (JOHN 4:10, 13–14)

A second time was at the Feast of Booths.

> **On the last day of the feast, the great day, Jesus stood up and cried out, "If anyone thirsts, let him come to Me and drink. Whoever believes in Me, as the Scripture has said, 'Out of his heart will flow rivers of living water.'" Now this He said about the Spirit, whom those who believed in Him were to receive, for as yet the Spirit had not been given, because Jesus was not yet glorified.** (JOHN 7:37–39)

Another came after Jesus had died on the cross.

> **But when they came to Jesus and saw that He was already dead, they did not break His legs. But one of the soldiers pierced His side with a spear, and at once there came out blood and water.** (JOHN 19:33–34)

Jesus is the temple of God who dwells among His people and poured out His Spirit on His disciples at Pentecost.

Daniel

◇◇◇◇◇◇◇◇◇◇◇◇◇◇◇◇◇◇◇◇

The prophet Daniel served the exiles during the same time Jeremiah and Ezekiel served as prophets, but his ministry took a slightly different path. While they were priests who became prophets, Daniel was a bright young man who was handpicked by his Babylonian captors to be trained to become a government official. While God was meeting His people's spiritual needs through Jeremiah and Ezekiel, He was guarding and protecting them from the whims of despots like Babylon's King Nebuchadnezzar through Daniel and his prophecies.

Daniel was exiled to Babylon in 597 BC at the same time Ezekiel was exiled. The Babylonians liked to take young, impressionable captives and train them so they could help incorporate the captive nations into the empire. Daniel was among the young Jews chosen to study the wisdom of the Babylonians so they could serve as the king's advisers, which the Persians called Magi. Daniel and three other Jewish youths, Shadrach, Meshach, and Abednego, clearly exceeded all the others. All four were given prominent positions in the local government.

❀ THE STONE THAT DEMOLISHED THE IMAGE ❀

Then one night, King Nebuchadnezzar had a troubling dream. The next morning, he summoned his wise men to interpret it. But he was well aware that his advisers could make up any interpretation in order to give it a favorable twist. He wouldn't know if their interpretation was correct until significant time had passed; therefore, if the dream was a warning from the gods and he didn't act on it immediately, the result could be disaster for his kingdom.

In order to be certain that he could rely on their honest interpretation, he did not tell them what he had dreamed. Instead, he commanded them to reveal both the dream and its interpretation. If they knew his dream accurately, he could be sure of their interpretation. Of course, his wise men were unable to tell him what he had dreamed. He became furious and ordered all his wise men to be executed.

When word reached Daniel, he requested time to seek God's answer, then reported to the king.

↝ Read Daniel 2:25–49.

God had given Daniel both Nebuchadnezzar's dream and its interpretation. After describing the dream in vivid detail, Daniel explained that the frightening image in the dream represented a combination of the world empires to come. King Nebuchadnezzar's Babylon was the head; a second empire would be its chest and arms; a third kingdom, its middle and thighs; and a fourth and final empire, its legs of iron and feet of iron mixed with clay.

Who is the stone that destroyed these kingdoms?

During Daniel's lifetime, the Babylonian Empire fell to the second in the dream, the Persian Empire. The four centuries between the close of the Old Testament and the beginning of the New saw the third and fourth kingdoms: the Greek (or Macedonian) Empire under Alexander the Great, and the Roman Empire.

Each of these world empires had its day in the sun before it fell to the next. Finally, the Roman Empire fell to barbarians, and yet the Christian Church remained and will continue to stand until Christ's return. When Jesus was on trial before the Roman governor Pontius Pilate, He made a great confession about His kingship and His kingdom.

> So Pilate entered his headquarters again and called Jesus and said to Him, "Are You the King of the Jews?" Jesus answered, "Do you say this of your own accord, or did others say it to you about Me?" Pilate answered, "Am I a Jew? Your own nation and the chief priests have delivered You over to me. What have You done?" Jesus answered, "My kingdom is not of this world. If My kingdom were of this world, My servants would have been fighting, that I might not be delivered over to the Jews. But My kingdom is not from the world." Then Pilate said to Him, "So You are a king?" Jesus answered, "You say that I am a king. For this purpose I was born and for this purpose I have come into the world—to bear witness to the truth. Everyone who is of the truth listens to My voice." (JOHN 18:33–37)

Forty days after His resurrection, when Jesus ascended into heaven, He took His place at the Father's right hand with all nations and kingdoms on earth subject to Him. He continues to rule all things in heaven and on earth for the benefit of His Bride, the Church.

❀ DANIEL IN THE LIONS' DEN ❀

Daniel continued to be very influential and prominent in the Babylonian Empire. Even after Babylon was conquered by the Persians, Daniel retained a high position in that new government. He was made administrator over one-third of the Persian Empire and so distinguished himself over the other two rulers that Persian King Darius decided to promote him over the entire kingdom. The other Persian officials, out of jealousy, sought a way to destroy Daniel.

* Read Daniel 6:6–18.

Perhaps no other account in the Old Testament has as many parallels to the Passion of Christ as does the account of Daniel in the lions' den.

Just as the Persian officials pressured King Darius to condemn Daniel to the lions' den, the Jewish religious authorities pressured Pontius Pilate to condemn Jesus to death by crucifixion.

> Then Pilate took Jesus and flogged Him. And the soldiers twisted together a crown of thorns and put it on His head and arrayed Him in a purple robe. They came up to Him, saying, "Hail, King of the Jews!" and struck Him with their hands. Pilate went out again and said to them, "See, I am bringing Him out to you that you may know that I find no guilt in Him." So Jesus came out, wearing the crown of thorns and the purple robe. Pilate said to them, "Behold the man!" When the chief priests and the officers saw Him, they cried out, "Crucify Him, crucify Him!" Pilate said to them, "Take Him yourselves and crucify Him, for I find no guilt in Him." The Jews answered him, "We have a law, and according to that law He ought to die because He has made Himself the Son of God." When Pilate heard this statement, he was even more afraid. He entered his headquarters again and said to Jesus, "Where are You from?" But Jesus gave him no answer. So Pilate said to Him, "You will not speak to me? Do You not know that I have authority to release You and authority to crucify You?" Jesus answered him, "You would have no authority over Me at all unless it had been given you from above. Therefore he who delivered Me over to you has the greater sin."

> From then on Pilate sought to release Him, but the Jews cried out, "If you release this man, you are not Caesar's friend. Everyone who makes himself a king opposes Caesar." So when Pilate heard these words, he brought Jesus out and sat down on the judgment seat at a place called The Stone Pavement, and in Aramaic Gabbatha. Now it was the day of Preparation of the Passover. It was about the sixth hour. He said to the Jews, "Behold your King!" They cried

out, "Away with Him, away with Him, crucify Him!" Pilate said to them, "Shall I crucify your King?" The chief priests answered, "We have no king but Caesar." So he delivered Him over to them to be crucified. (JOHN 19:1–16)

Finally, both Persian King Darius and the Roman governor Pontius Pilate caved in to the pressures of the officials and condemned innocent Daniel and Jesus to death. Jesus was hung on a tree until He died, then buried in a tomb, which was closed with a great stone. Daniel was lowered into the lions' den, and its opening was closed with a great stone. As far as his enemies were concerned, Daniel was dead and they had seen the last of him.

But then, early in the morning, King Darius rushed out to what he thought was Daniel's tomb and ordered the stone to be removed. Daniel came out of the lions' den safe and sound.

⁕ Read Daniel 6:19–23.

This sounds similar to Mary Magdalene's experience on that Sunday morning after Jesus died and was buried.

Now on the first day of the week Mary Magdalene came to the tomb early, while it was still dark, and saw that the stone had been taken away from the tomb. So she ran and went to Simon Peter and the other disciple, the one whom Jesus loved, and said to them, "They have taken the Lord out of the tomb, and we do not know where they have laid Him." So Peter went out with the other disciple, and they were going toward the tomb. Both of them were running together, but the other disciple outran Peter and reached the tomb first. And stooping to look in, he saw the linen cloths lying there, but he did not go in. Then Simon Peter came, following him, and went into the tomb. He saw the linen cloths lying there, and the face cloth, which had been on Jesus' head, not lying with the linen cloths but folded up in a place by itself. Then the other disciple, who had reached the tomb first, also went in, and he saw and believed; for as yet they did not understand the Scripture, that He must rise from the dead. Then the disciples went back to their homes.

But Mary stood weeping outside the tomb, and as she wept she stooped to look into the tomb. And she saw two angels in white, sitting where the body of Jesus had lain, one at the head and one at the feet. They said to her, "Woman, why are you weeping?" She said to them, "They have taken away my Lord, and I do not know where they have laid Him." Having said this, she turned around and saw Jesus standing, but she did not know that it was Jesus. Jesus said to her, "Woman, why are you weeping? Whom are you seeking?" Supposing Him to be the gardener, she said to Him, "Sir, if you have carried Him away, tell me where you have laid Him, and I will take Him away." Jesus said to her, "Mary." She turned and said to Him in Aramaic, "Rabboni!" (which means Teacher). Jesus said to her, "Do not cling to Me, for I have not yet ascended to the Father; but go to My brothers and say to them, 'I am ascending to My Father and your Father, to My God and your God.'" Mary Magdalene went and announced to the disciples, "I have seen the Lord"—and that He had said these things to her. (JOHN 20:1–18)

❈ CHRIST'S ETERNAL KINGDOM ❈

After Daniel 6, the remaining chapters consist of visions God gave Daniel regarding the time between the close of the Old Testament and the coming of the promised Savior at the start of the New Testament. His first vision set the wider political context with the same four empires that Nebuchadnezzar had seen in his dream in Daniel 2 (Babylon, Persia, Macedonia, and Rome). And just as in that dream, the Christ is mentioned during the time of the Romans.

❖ Read Daniel 7:9–14.

Who is the "Ancient of Days" (v. 9)?

This was an extremely important passage for the coming generation of Jews after the close of the Old Testament. They could watch Daniel's prophecies unfold as Babylon fell to the Persians, Persia fell to Alexander the Great and the Macedonians, and Macedonia fell to the Romans. Though Israel was a tiny nation in that age of empires, God's kingdom, the believers, is supreme—and the only one that will last until that day when Christ will return in power to judge the nations. On Tuesday of Holy Week, Jesus taught His disciples about the day He will return to judge the world.

> **Immediately after the tribulation of those days the sun will be darkened, and the moon will not give its light, and the stars will fall from heaven, and the powers of the heavens will be shaken. Then will appear in heaven the sign of the Son of Man, and then all the tribes of the earth will mourn, and they will see the Son of Man coming on the clouds of heaven with power and great glory. And He will send out His angels with a loud trumpet call, and they will gather His elect from the four winds, from one end of heaven to the other. (Matthew 24:29–31)**

❋ THE TIME OF CHRIST'S DEATH IS SET ❋

As we look back at the Jews who did not recognize the visitation of Jesus, we may get the impression that it was easy to miss Him, because no one would know exactly when the Christ would come. But through Daniel, God identified a very clear time frame within which the Christ would be cut off, suffer, and die.

↝ Read Daniel 9:24–26.

Where is Jesus in this mysterious passage?

Amazingly, in verse 25, Daniel prophesied the rebuilding of Jerusalem and the temple, which is recorded in Ezra, and the rebuilding of the walls of Jerusalem, which is recorded in Nehemiah. The "prince who is to come" would be the Roman emperor whose armies would destroy Jerusalem and burn down the temple in AD 70.

Therefore Daniel made clear the time frame within which Jesus would come to save us from our sins—between the rebuilding of the temple and its destruction by the Romans. This is yet another compelling reason that Jesus alone could be the true Messiah, and any Jews still waiting for the coming of the Messiah are waiting in vain. The time Daniel prophesied has come and gone long ago. Jesus of Nazareth was the promised Christ who has already come.

Daniel is an amazing book. Not only did it give a prophetic summary of the political situation in Canaan for the next four hundred years and beyond; it also laid out the time in which the Savior would come. And it pointed out the Savior's great sacrifice on the cross and the Romans who put an end to all the Jewish sacrifices when they destroyed the temple in AD 70. It even closes with the resurrection of all the dead on the Last Day and the judgment of believers and unbelievers.

❀ CONCLUSION ❀

The major prophets wrote many words to convict the people of Judah for their sins and call them to repent and trust the Lord and His promise of salvation. Their words also call out to us to turn from our sins and cling to Jesus Christ, our Savior, who has suffered in our place and risen victorious over sin and death.

❀ CLOSING PRAYER ❀

Lord God, heavenly Father, the prophecies regarding Your Son, Jesus, and His coming are amazingly specific and clear. Enlighten the hearts and minds of the Jews who still await His coming, and bring them to Him in repentance and sincere faith. Increase our confidence and certainty that Jesus is the Christ, Your Son. In Jesus' name. Amen.

SESSION 8

❀ OPENING PRAYER ❀

Lord Jesus, in this last session, we will work through the so-called "minor prophets." Yet we only use that title because their works are shorter, not because they are less important than those we have read before. Show us that each of these books is precious and valuable because each points us to Your coming, and to the salvation You accomplished for all of us. Amen.

Hosea

M any prophets in the Old Testament used the picture of marriage to speak about the relationship between God and His people. In the Book of Hosea, God took this to an extreme. He commanded the prophet Hosea to marry a promiscuous woman. When she was unfaithful to him, God commanded Hosea to set aside his wrath and pride and go to the other man. Hosea ransomed her and took her back to himself. Through the prophet's own experience, God exposed Israel's waywardness, called on them to repent, and promised His forgiveness. The prophet gave many warnings of the destruction and punishment to come if they refused to repent, and he closed with God's plea for His people to receive His forgiveness and restoration.

❁ GOD CALLS BACK HIS WAYWARD WIFE ❁

In the Gospels, Jesus revealed Himself as the Groom and His Bride as the Church. Many of Jesus' parables spoke of the wedding feast a king (God the Father) holds for his son (Jesus Christ), and these prefigure Judgment Day, when Christ will come to bring us to live with Him in paradise forever.

◦ Read Hosea 2:14–23.

Where do we see Jesus in this passage?

In Matthew 25, Jesus gave a parable where He is the Groom and we are the attendants awaiting His arrival on Judgment Day.

Then the kingdom of heaven will be like ten virgins who took their lamps and went to meet the bridegroom. Five of them were foolish, and five were wise. For when the foolish took their lamps, they took no oil with them, but the wise took flasks of oil with their lamps. As the bridegroom was delayed, they all became drowsy and slept. But at midnight there was a cry, "Here is the bridegroom! Come out to meet him." Then all those virgins rose and trimmed their lamps. And the foolish said to the wise, "Give us some of your oil, for our lamps are going out." But the wise answered, saying, "Since there will not be enough for us and for you, go rather to the dealers and buy for yourselves." And while they were going to buy, the bridegroom came, and those who were ready went in with him to the marriage feast, and the door was shut. Afterward the other virgins came also, saying, "Lord, lord, open to us." But he answered, "Truly, I say to you, I do not know you." Watch therefore, for you know neither the day nor the hour. (MATTHEW 25:1–13)

❋ JESUS' RESURRECTION FORETOLD ❋

Hosea called for the faithless people of Israel to repent of their sins and return to God, who promised to forgive and restore them. God's plan to restore us included sending His Son to suffer and die and rise again. Hosea prophesied that resurrection on the third day in chapter 6.

⤝ Read Hosea 6:1–2.

> *Where do we see Jesus' resurrection?*
>
> ....
> ....
> ....
> ....

Jesus used that very same language when He appeared to His disciples in the locked Upper Room the night after His resurrection.

> Then He said to them, "These are My words that I spoke to you while I was still with you, that everything written about Me in the Law of Moses and the Prophets and the Psalms must be fulfilled." Then He opened their minds to understand the Scriptures, and said to them, "Thus it is written, that the Christ should suffer and on the third day rise from the dead, and that repentance for the forgiveness of sins should be proclaimed in His name to all nations, beginning from Jerusalem. You are witnesses of these things."
> (LUKE 24:44–48)

Joel

All prophets warned God's people of their sins, calling them to repent before God's judgment came upon them and consumed them. Different prophets used different pictures or images to represent that judgment.

Joel compared it to a locust infestation. Locusts devastated ancient agricultural nations like Israel that lived from one harvest to the next. A huge swarm of locusts could strip all the vegetation from the fields, leaving nothing behind but starvation and death.

Joel used this catastrophe to illustrate and warn against God's devastating judgment on unrepented sins and to plead for the people of Judah to repent and receive God's forgiveness before it was too late.

On a brighter note, Joel prophesied that Jesus would pour out the Holy Spirit upon His faithful disciples on Pentecost in chapter 2:

> And it shall come to pass afterward, that I will pour out
> My Spirit on all flesh; your sons and your daughters shall
> prophesy, your old men shall dream dreams, and your
> young men shall see visions. Even on the male and female
> servants in those days I will pour out My Spirit. (JOEL 2:28–29)

Jesus spoke about this to His disciples at the Last Supper the night before He died.

> But I have said these things to you, that when their hour
> comes you may remember that I told them to you.
>
> I did not say these things to you from the beginning,
> because I was with you. But now I am going to Him who
> sent Me, and none of you asks Me, "Where are You going?"
> But because I have said these things to you, sorrow has
> filled your heart. Nevertheless, I tell you the truth: it is to
> your advantage that I go away, for if I do not go away, the
> Helper will not come to you. But if I go, I will send Him to
> you. And when He comes, He will convict the world con-
> cerning sin and righteousness and judgment: concerning
> sin, because they do not believe in Me; concerning righ-
> teousness, because I go to the Father, and you will see Me no
> longer; concerning judgment, because the ruler of this world
> is judged.
>
> I still have many things to say to you, but you cannot bear
> them now. When the Spirit of truth comes, He will guide
> you into all the truth, for He will not speak on His own

authority, but whatever He hears He will speak, and He will declare to you the things that are to come. He will glorify Me, for He will take what is Mine and declare it to you. All that the Father has is Mine; therefore I said that He will take what is Mine and declare it to you. (JOHN 16:4–15)

Amos

✕✕✕✕✕✕✕✕✕✕✕✕✕✕✕✕✕✕✕

Amos was a fiery prophet, sent from Judah to warn Israel of total destruction if they did not repent. He exposed their excess, greed, idolatry, and injustice. God would loose the savage Assyrians upon them like a lion and send them into captivity.

❀ THE BOOTH OF DAVID ❀

This passage gives a rather obscure but revealing prophecy of the coming of the Christ. David's palace, His very kingship, would become nothing but a booth, a lowly hut, weak, decrepit, and fallen.

This happened when the Babylonian king Nebuchadnezzar conquered Jerusalem and dethroned the descendants of David. Elsewhere in the Old Testament, David's fallen kingdom is described as a tree that is cut down—the stump of Jesse (David's father). Yet out of that stump would spring forth a tender shoot.

⤖ Read Amos 9:11.

How does a booth represent Jesus Christ?

Jesus seldom spoke about His poverty, but in one passage He did mention it.

> **Now when Jesus saw a crowd around Him, He gave orders to go over to the other side. And a scribe came up and said to Him, "Teacher, I will follow You wherever You go." And Jesus said to him, "Foxes have holes, and birds of the air have nests, but the Son of Man has nowhere to lay His head."** (MATTHEW 8:18–20)

David had sincerely wanted to build a temple—a permanent house for God rather than the tent in which His ark had dwelt since Moses' time. But God promised to David that one of his descendants would be the promised Christ. That Messiah would make David's house, or line, permanent by rising from the dead and taking His own permanent place reigning at the Father's right hand for all eternity.

Obadiah

◇◇◇◇◇◇◇◇◇◇◇◇◇◇◇◇◇◇◇◇◇◇◇◇◇◇

In Obadiah, God confronted the people of Edom, who took delight in the destruction of Jerusalem and the exile of Judah. The Edomites were descendants of Jacob's brother, Esau, and they lived in perpetual hatred of Israel. When Babylon came against Jerusalem, the Edomites took great delight in watching Jerusalem's fall. They mocked the people of Judah and even betrayed the Jewish fugitives who had fled to them, turning them over to the Babylonians who were pursuing them.

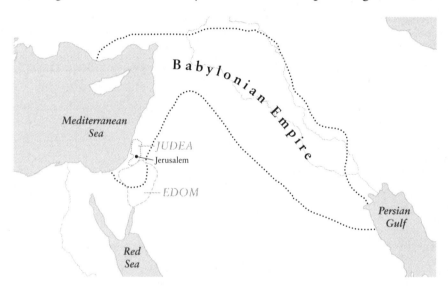

⌁ Read Obadiah 10–14.

How can we see Jesus in this passage?

We see Jesus' anguish most clearly in Obadiah when we compare the hostility and cruelty of the Edomites to that of Jesus' enemies who sought His death and gloated over Him, delighted in His distress, and mocked and scoffed at Him as He hung on the cross, suffering terribly.

> And the people stood by, watching, but the rulers scoffed at Him, saying, "He saved others; let Him save Himself, if He is the Christ of God, His Chosen One!" The soldiers also mocked Him, coming up and offering Him sour wine and saying, "If You are the King of the Jews, save Yourself!" There was also an inscription over Him, "This is the King of the Jews."
>
> One of the criminals who were hanged railed at Him, saying, "Are You not the Christ? Save Yourself and us!"
> (LUKE 23:35–39)

Yet just as God restored the captives to return and rebuild Jerusalem, the Father raised Jesus to life on the third day, and He will return as the glorious King of kings on the Last Day to judge the world and give eternal life to all believers.

Jonah

In the Book of Jonah, God sent the prophet to the wicked city of Nineveh, capital of the ungodly Assyrian Empire, to call them to repent and amend their violent lives. There are amazing parallels between Jonah's life and Jesus' life.

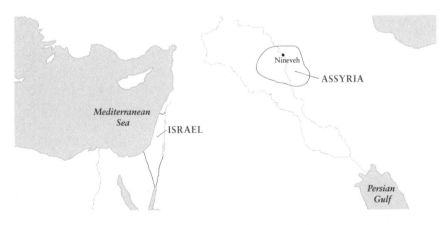

❋ ASLEEP IN A STORM ❋

Though Jesus' life was parallel in many ways to Jonah's, in many ways they were traveling in different directions. When God sent Jesus to the lost sheep of Israel, Jesus joyfully went. When God sent Jonah to the lost people of Nineveh, Jonah ran in the other direction. Both ended up on a boat, sleeping through a storm.

⤙ Read Jonah 1.

Jesus' experience is strangely similar.

> On that day, when evening had come, He said to them, "Let us go across to the other side." And leaving the crowd, they took Him with them in the boat, just as He was. And other boats were with Him. And a great windstorm arose, and the waves were breaking into the boat, so that the boat was already filling. But He was in the stern, asleep on the cushion. And they woke Him and said to Him, "Teacher, do You not care that we are perishing?" And He awoke and rebuked the wind and said to the sea, "Peace! Be still!" And the wind ceased, and there was a great calm. He said to them, "Why are you so afraid? Have you still no faith?" And they were filled with great fear and said to one another, "Who then is this, that even the wind and the sea obey Him?" (MARK 4:35–41)

How were their experiences similar?

Jesus took it a step further. In Matthew 12, He made a connection between the time Jonah spent in the fish with the time He would spend in the grave after His crucifixion.

> Then some of the scribes and Pharisees answered Him, saying, "Teacher, we wish to see a sign from You." But He answered them, "An evil and adulterous generation seeks for a sign, but no sign will be given to it except the sign of the prophet Jonah. For just as Jonah was three days and three nights in the belly of the great fish, so will the Son of Man be three days and three nights in the heart of the earth."
> (MATTHEW 12:38–40)

❈ GREATER THAN JONAH ❈

After three days and nights, the fish spit Jonah out onto the shore. He obeyed God and preached in Nineveh, with rousing success. The people repented and turned from their wickedness, and God spared the city.

But once again, we see how different Jonah and Jesus really were.

✦ Read Jonah 4.

> *What was the difference between Jonah's reaction and Jesus' reaction?*

Thinking of Jonah's hatred for Nineveh, Jesus warned the people,

> The men of Nineveh will rise up at the judgment with this generation and condemn it, for they repented at the preaching of Jonah, and behold, something greater than Jonah is here. (MATTHEW 12:41)

Micah

◇◇◇◇◇◇◇◇◇◇◇◇◇◇◇◇◇◇◇◇

Micah confronted the sin of Judah and Israel, especially the leaders who let the nations fall into ruin while they indulged their sinful desires. In the middle of his book, Micah revealed God's mercy and promised blessings upon God's faithful people. He especially spoke of the birthplace of the coming Savior.

ISRAEL

Jerusalem
Bethlehem

JUDEA

❀ BETHLEHEM EPHRATHAH ❀

↝ Read Micah 5:2–5.

What is so important about this prophecy of Jesus' birthplace?

Matthew wrote his Gospel primarily for Jews, to show that Jesus had fulfilled all the Old Testament prophecies. His account of the visit of the Wise Men and King Herod's murderous reaction in Matthew 2 was actually critical for Matthew's purposes.

> Now after Jesus was born in Bethlehem of Judea in the days of Herod the king, behold, wise men from the east came to Jerusalem, saying, "Where is He who has been born king of the Jews? For we saw His star when it rose and have come to worship Him." When Herod the king heard this, he was troubled, and all Jerusalem with him; and assembling all the chief priests and scribes of the people, he inquired of them where the Christ was to be born. They told him, "In Bethlehem of Judea, for so it is written by the prophet:
>
> "'And you, O Bethlehem, in the land of Judah, are by no means least among the rulers of Judah; for from you shall come a ruler who will shepherd My people Israel.'"
>
> Then Herod summoned the wise men secretly and ascertained from them what time the star had appeared. And he sent them to Bethlehem, saying, "Go and search diligently for the child, and when you have found Him, bring me word, that I too may come and worship Him." After listening to the king, they went on their way. And behold, the star that they had seen when it rose went before them until it came to rest over the place where the child was. When they saw the star, they rejoiced exceedingly with great joy. And going into the house they saw the child with Mary His mother, and they fell down and worshiped Him. Then, opening their treasures, they offered Him gifts, gold and frankincense and myrrh. And being warned in a dream not to return to Herod, they departed to their own country by another way.
>
> Now when they had departed, behold, an angel of the Lord appeared to Joseph in a dream and said, "Rise, take the child and His mother, and flee to Egypt, and remain there until I tell you, for Herod is about to search for the child,

to destroy Him." And he rose and took the child and His
mother by night and departed to Egypt and remained there
until the death of Herod. This was to fulfill what the Lord
had spoken by the prophet, "Out of Egypt I called My son."

Then Herod, when he saw that he had been tricked by the
wise men, became furious, and he sent and killed all the
male children in Bethlehem and in all that region who were
two years old or under, according to the time that he had
ascertained from the wise men. (MATTHEW 2:1–16)

After Jesus' death, resurrection, and ascension, one of the great
stumbling blocks Jews faced in coming to faith was Micah's prophecy
that the Christ would be born in Bethlehem. After all, Jesus was known
as "Jesus of Nazareth." Many Jews flatly refused to believe, because
they thought He should have been "Jesus of Bethlehem."

So Matthew's account of the Wise Men explains how Jesus was
actually born in Bethlehem as Micah foretold, but grew up in Nazareth
because of Joseph and Mary having to flee King Herod.

Nahum

◇◇◇◇◇◇◇◇◇◇◇◇◇◇◇◇◇◇◇◇◇◇◇◇◇◇◇◇◇

Nahum brought comfort to the believers afflicted by the brutal Assyrian
Empire. You may remember from the Historical Books that Assyria
conquered the Northern Kingdom of Israel and swept down through
Judah, capturing every fortified city before laying siege to Jerusalem.
It was during this harrowing time that the prophet Nahum brought
the promise of God's deliverance.

That deliverance was given when God sent an angel, who decimated
the Assyrian army and they fled back to their homeland. But it points
ahead to an even greater deliverance, when God's own Son, Jesus,
walked the mountains of Galilee.

❀ THE BRINGER OF GOOD NEWS AND PEACE ❀

↝ Read Nahum 1:12–15.

> *How can verse 15 apply to Jesus?*

That evening at sundown they brought to Him all who were sick or oppressed by demons. And the whole city was gathered together at the door. And He healed many who were sick with various diseases, and cast out many demons. And He would not permit the demons to speak, because they knew Him.

And rising very early in the morning, while it was still dark, He departed and went out to a desolate place, and there He prayed. And Simon and those who were with Him searched for Him, and they found Him and said to Him, "Everyone is looking for You." And He said to them, "Let us go on to the next towns, that I may preach there also, for that is why I came out." And He went throughout all Galilee, preaching in their synagogues and casting out demons. (MARK 1:32–39)

Through His Word in the New Testament, Jesus Christ brings hope and the assurance of victory over sin, Satan, death, and hell to all His own.

Habakkuk

In Habakkuk, the prophet asked God why He tolerated the injustice being done to His faithful and did not answer their prayers for deliverance.

❈ THE WICKED SURROUND THE RIGHTEOUS ❈

⤝ Read Habakkuk 1:2–4.

How can this passage remind us of Jesus?

Jesus was a victim of that injustice in the false trials and abuse He suffered at the hands of the Jewish religious leaders when they handed Him over to Pilate and pressured Pilate to crucify Him. The injustice and torment continued as they surrounded and mocked Him on the cross.

And those who passed by derided Him, wagging their heads and saying, "Aha! You who would destroy the temple and rebuild it in three days, save Yourself, and come down from the cross!" So also the chief priests with the scribes mocked Him to one another, saying, "He saved others; He cannot save Himself. Let the Christ, the King of Israel, come down now from the cross that we may see and believe." Those who were crucified with Him also reviled Him. (MARK 15:29–32)

Jesus had complete faith in His Father, trusting that at the right time, God would vindicate Him (prove Him to be in the right). He was so confident in His Father's faithfulness that He could pray, "Father, forgive them, for they know not what they do" (Luke 23:34), and, "Father, into Your hands I commit My spirit!" (Luke 23:46).

❈ I WILL JOY IN THE GOD OF MY SALVATION ❈

In answer to Habakkuk's complaint of injustice in Jerusalem, God promised to bring in the Babylonians to destroy Jerusalem and end the injustice taking place there. When Habakkuk asked how God could bring in such a corrupt and wicked nation to punish Israel, God answered that in time, Babylon would likewise be punished. Trusting God's promise, Habakkuk could face the coming darkness with faith and confidence.

⤳ Read Habakkuk 3:17–19.

> *In the midst of great poverty and suffering, how could the prophet find joy and peace?*

Notice that he called the Lord "the God of my salvation." Jesus spoke about that peace the night before He died.

> "Let not your hearts be troubled. Believe in God; believe also in Me. In My Father's house are many rooms. If it were not so, would I have told you that I go to prepare a place for you? And if I go and prepare a place for you, I will come again and will take you to Myself, that where I am you may be also. And you know the way to where I am going." Thomas said to Him, "Lord, we do not know where You are going. How can we know the way?" Jesus said to him, "I am the way, and the truth, and the life. No one comes to the

**Father except through Me. If you had known Me, you would
have known My Father also. From now on you do know
Him and have seen Him."** (JOHN 14:1–7)

Jesus is that Savior who left His place in heaven; lived His earthly
life; suffered affliction, mistreatment, and death; and thereby saved us
from our sins. He is the God of our salvation, and that salvation makes
us joyful, even when we are in the midst of great suffering.

Zephaniah

The Book of Zephaniah focuses on the day of God's judgment, when He
will judge and punish all sinners. That day was foreshadowed often in the
Old Testament (e.g., Noah's flood, Sodom and Gomorrah's destruction,
Jerusalem's fall). But it is most clearly seen in the suffering and death
of Jesus on the cross, and the darkness that covered the land at that
time. Zephaniah warned his readers to repent and believe before the
Lord Jesus returns on that great day to judge the living and the dead.

❈ THE DAY OF THE LORD ❈

Zephaniah lived and prophesied at the same time as the prophet
Jeremiah. He described the terrifying moment when God will come
to judge His people. Its first fulfillment was when Babylon destroyed
Jerusalem. Its ultimate fulfillment will take place when Jesus returns.

⤳ Read Zephaniah 1:14–18.

Whenever we think of events of judgment in the Bible that give us
a glimpse of Judgment Day—the flood, the destruction of Sodom and
Gomorrah, the fall of Jerusalem, and so forth—it is also important to
remember our Savior's death on the cross.

> *How does this passage foreshadow Jesus' death on the cross?*
>
> _____
>
> _____
>
> _____
>
> _____
>
> _____

In truth, that was Judgment Day for all humans of every age because Jesus was carrying and paying for the sins of every human of all time as He hung on the cross. Because Jesus has already suffered the judgment we deserve, we need have no fear of the Judgment Day to come. But the Bible's warnings of Judgment Day are important reminders to us to not slip away from the teachings of Jesus and His great salvation. Why? Because everyone who faces that judgment without Christ will be condemned to never-ending suffering in hell.

❈ THE LORD YOUR GOD IS IN YOUR MIDST ❈

The Book of Zephaniah concludes with a beautiful description of the benefits our Lord Jesus won for us through His day of judgment on the cross.

◦ Read Zephaniah 3:11–20.

> *What does this passage tell us about the effects of Jesus' work on His Church?*
>
> _____
>
> _____
>
> _____
>
> _____
>
> _____

As Zephaniah reminds us about Judgment Day, he leads us to repent of our sins and take comfort from the salvation that is ours for the sake of Jesus Christ, our Lord.

Haggai

Haggai was one of the last prophets in the Old Testament (with Zechariah and Malachi). His ministry is mentioned along with Zechariah's in Ezra 5:1. God called him to encourage the exiles to resume rebuilding the temple after its construction had been halted by King Artaxerxes. The king gave this command after he received a letter from Judah's enemies, the Samaritans. After Artaxerxes died, Haggai called on the exiles to trust God and resume building without waiting for permission from the new king, Darius.

❀ THE LATTER GLORY OF THIS HOUSE ❀

Some of the older returned exiles had seen Solomon's temple and were very disillusioned with this replacement.

⮞ Read Haggai 2:1–9.

> *Why did this new temple seem like nothing to many of the old priests, Levites, and leaders of fathers' houses?*

The new temple, sometimes called "Zerubbabel's temple" after the prince of Judah who was governor of Jerusalem at the time, didn't have the gold, silver, and bronze with which Solomon's temple had been built. But through Haggai, God promised a greater glory for it than Solomon's temple ever had. This was because within the courts of this temple, Jesus Christ, the Son of God and promised Messiah, would come. A future generation would see Jesus Christ standing in these temple courts, preaching to the people and healing their sick. They would literally see God's Son standing in His Father's house, even cleansing and restoring it.

> **The Passover of the Jews was at hand, and Jesus went up to Jerusalem. In the temple He found those who were selling oxen and sheep and pigeons, and the money-changers sitting there. And making a whip of cords, He drove them all out of the temple, with the sheep and oxen. And He poured out the coins of the money-changers and overturned their tables. And He told those who sold the pigeons, "Take these things away; do not make My Father's house a house of trade."** (John 2:13–16)

Zechariah

◇◇◇◇◇◇◇◇◇◇◇◇◇◇◇◇◇◇◇◇◇◇◇◇◇◇◇◇◇◇◇

About three months after Haggai began encouraging the exiles to resume construction on the new temple, God raised up Zechariah as a second witness to preach the same thing.

But along with his encouragement for the returned exiles to again take up the rebuilding of the temple, Zechariah gives us some unique glances at Jesus Christ, especially in the events of Holy Week, that week that began with His triumphal entry on Palm Sunday, saw His suffering and death on Good Friday, and witnessed His glorious resurrection the following Sunday, Easter Day.

❁ IN A SINGLE DAY ❁

In Zechariah 3, God defended the high priest Joshua against Satan's accusations. Then Zechariah announced the single day in which God would remove the iniquities of the land.

-⊷ Read Zechariah 3:8–10.

> *What does this passage reveal about the work of Jesus Christ?*

Verse 8 identifies the promised Savior as "the Branch." We have seen this title for the promised Messiah in previous prophetic books. This identifies the Christ as a descendant of David and his father, Jesse. Isaiah had given this prophecy of the shoot that would spring from the stump of Jesse (Isaiah 11:1). Zechariah 3:9 describes the effect of Jesus' suffering and death on Good Friday: "I will remove the iniquity of this land in a single day."

❀ YOUR KING IS COMING TO YOU ❀

Beginning in chapter 9, Zechariah gave some amazingly detailed prophecies about Jesus' final week, beginning with Palm Sunday.

-⊷ Read Zechariah 9:9–11.

> *What event from Jesus' life was Zechariah prophesying?*

The Gospel of Matthew quotes this passage to show Jesus fulfilled this prophecy.

Now when they drew near to Jerusalem and came to Bethphage, to the Mount of Olives, then Jesus sent two

disciples, saying to them, "Go into the village in front of you, and immediately you will find a donkey tied, and a colt with her. Untie them and bring them to Me. If anyone says anything to you, you shall say, 'The Lord needs them,' and he will send them at once." This took place to fulfill what was spoken by the prophet, saying,

"Say to the daughter of Zion, 'Behold, your king is coming to you, humble, and mounted on a donkey, on a colt, the foal of a beast of burden.'"

The disciples went and did as Jesus had directed them. They brought the donkey and the colt and put on them their cloaks, and He sat on them. Most of the crowd spread their cloaks on the road, and others cut branches from the trees and spread them on the road. And the crowds that went before Him and that followed Him were shouting, "Hosanna to the Son of David! Blessed is He who comes in the name of the Lord! Hosanna in the highest!" (MATTHEW 21:1–9)

❋ JUDAS'S BETRAYAL PROPHESIED ❋

Then, in chapter 11, Zechariah predicted details of Judas's betrayal of Jesus.

✦ Read Zechariah 11:12–13.

> *Which details of Judas's betrayal did Zechariah prophesy?*
>
> _____
>
> _____
>
> _____
>
> _____
>
> _____

This is a fascinating collection of various events.

Then one of the twelve, whose name was Judas Iscariot, went to the chief priests and said, "What will you give me if

I deliver Him over to you?" And they paid him thirty pieces of silver. And from that moment he sought an opportunity to betray Him. (MATTHEW 26:14–16)

While [Jesus] was still speaking, Judas came, one of the twelve, and with him a great crowd with swords and clubs, from the chief priests and the elders of the people. Now the betrayer had given them a sign, saying, "The one I will kiss is the man; seize Him." And he came up to Jesus at once and said, "Greetings, Rabbi!" And he kissed Him. Jesus said to him, "Friend, do what you came to do." Then they came up and laid hands on Jesus and seized Him. (MATTHEW 26:47–50)

Then when Judas, His betrayer, saw that Jesus was condemned, he changed his mind and brought back the thirty pieces of silver to the chief priests and the elders, saying, "I have sinned by betraying innocent blood." They said, "What is that to us? See to it yourself." And throwing down the pieces of silver into the temple, he departed, and he went and hanged himself. But the chief priests, taking the pieces of silver, said, "It is not lawful to put them into the treasury, since it is blood money." So they took counsel and bought with them the potter's field as a burial place for strangers. Therefore that field has been called the Field of Blood to this day. Then was fulfilled what had been spoken by the prophet Jeremiah, saying, "And they took the thirty pieces of silver, the price of Him on whom a price had been set by some of the sons of Israel, and they gave them for the potter's field, as the Lord directed me." (MATTHEW 27:3–10)

When we consider Zechariah's prophecy, it is clear to see he was prophesying events from Jesus' Passion.

❀ THEY SHALL MOURN FOR HIM ❀

Zechariah gave one more incredible Holy Week prophecy, fulfilled on Mount Calvary, where Jesus was crucified.

↪ Read Zechariah 12:10–13:1.

What events from Jesus' Passion was Zechariah prophesying?

Since it was the day of Preparation, and so that the bodies would not remain on the cross on the Sabbath (for that Sabbath was a high day), the Jews asked Pilate that their legs might be broken and that they might be taken away. So the soldiers came and broke the legs of the first, and of the other who had been crucified with Him. But when they came to Jesus and saw that He was already dead, they did not break His legs. But one of the soldiers pierced His side with a spear, and at once there came out blood and water. He who saw it has borne witness—his testimony is true, and he knows that he is telling the truth—that you also may believe. For these things took place that the Scripture might be fulfilled: "Not one of His bones will be broken." And again another Scripture says, "They will look on Him whom they have pierced." (JOHN 19:31–37)

All believers who look at the Son of God hanging on the cross, suffering for their sins, will mourn and grieve over their sins in true repentance. And from the spear that pierced His side, a fountain opened to cleanse us from our sin and guilt as water and blood rushed out of His body (v. 34).

Malachi

Malachi was the last prophet to write in the Old Testament. He wrote after the completion of the temple, and he included two prophecies about the coming of Jesus Christ.

❀ THE MESSENGER OF THE COVENANT ❀

In the first two chapters, Malachi addressed the corruption that had crept into the offerings and worship in the newly restored temple. Then, in chapter 3, he turned to future events, the day the Christ would stand in those very temple courts.

❧ Read Malachi 3:1–4.

Who were the two messengers Malachi mentions?

Jesus is called "the messenger of the covenant" because He brought a new covenant, or testament. He is Eve's "offspring" (Genesis 3:15) who would fulfill God's righteous plan and destroy the work of Satan. He brought a covenant of pure grace—forgiveness and peace—not on the basis of human works but on the basis of His perfect life and His innocent suffering and death for us.

❀ ELIJAH THE PROPHET ❀

Malachi ended his book with a thrilling promise.

❧ Read Malachi 4:5–6.

Whom did Malachi mean by "Elijah the prophet"?

John's message was similar to Elijah's message, calling on Israel to repent of their sins.

And the disciples asked [Jesus], "Then why do the scribes
say that first Elijah must come?" He answered, "Elijah does
come, and he will restore all things. But I tell you that Elijah
has already come, and they did not recognize him, but did
to him whatever they pleased. So also the Son of Man will
certainly suffer at their hands." Then the disciples under-
stood that He was speaking to them of John the Baptist.
(MATTHEW 17:10–13)

❈ CONCLUSION ❈

It is such a thrilling way to end the Old Testament. Christ's coming
was about four hundred years away. For those four centuries, the last
word of the last voice that echoed over time was Malachi's promise of
the coming of John. How stirring it must have been when word began
spreading that a prophet like Elijah was at the Jordan River, baptizing
and preaching. The time of the Messiah who had been promised from
the beginning to the end of the Old Testament had finally come.

❈ CLOSING PRAYER ❈

*Lord Jesus Christ, from Genesis through Malachi, we
read of Your great work on behalf of Your people.
Thank You for coming to live among us as a human, for
teaching us about the kingdom of Your Father, and for
laying down Your life to take away the sins of the world.
Through Your death and resurrection You have opened
the kingdom of heaven to all believers. Strengthen us in
faith by Your Holy Spirit, that we may share the Good
News of Your salvation and look forward to the day
when You will return to judge the living and dead and
establish Your kingdom forever. Amen.*

Answer Key

❀ SESSION 1 ❀

How does it transform our approach to Christmas when we realize the baby lying in the manger was actually the eternal Son of God, through whom everything was created?

> It can fill us with a deep awe and appreciation that Jesus was willing to leave His glorious throne in heaven to live among us—to share the joys and pains of earthly life, save us from our sins, and begin reclaiming His fallen creation.

Why is Jesus' Baptism so significant?

> His Baptism empowers our Baptism to take away our sins, make us God's children, and give us the Holy Spirit.

What did Jesus mean when He said "It is finished" on the cross?

> He meant that He had paid for all our sins in full. As a result, God is forever at peace with us for Jesus' sake.

What parts of Jesus' life are most familiar to you? Which parts are a bit unclear?

> Participants' answers will vary.

What difference does it make to you to know that Jesus was intimately involved in the creation of our world and the first humans?

> Participants' responses will vary.

What solution did God declare for humanity's fall into sin?

The offspring, or child, of the woman would "bruise . . . the head" of the serpent who had tempted Eve to sin; that is, He would destroy Satan.

Why should we see the story of the great flood and Noah's ark as more than a mythical children's story?

Since Jesus treated it as a historical fact, we should too. It also reminds us that judgment will fall again upon earth when Christ returns, and none will be able to escape it except through Spirit-given faith in Jesus, our Savior.

Where do we find the promise of the Christ in these three verses?

The fourth promise, the last phrase in verse 3, is the promise "in you all the families of the earth shall be blessed."

Why did Sarah laugh at such good news?

After waiting so long, Sarah had concluded it was impossible for her to become pregnant. She laughed in disbelief.

How is this account similar to John 3:16, "God so loved the world, that He gave His only Son"?

This event foreshadowed Jesus' death on the cross. As Abraham was willing to offer his only son (from Sarah) whom he loved, so on the cross, God the Father offered His only-begotten Son, whom He loved.

What made Jacob realize he was wrestling with the Lord Himself?

When the stranger touched Jacob's hip and put it out of joint, Jacob realized it was Christ. By asking Him to bless him, Jacob was showing he believed the stranger was God Himself.

How was Joseph's story similar to the story of Jesus' life?

Joseph served as a "type," or example, of Jesus.

❀ SESSION 2 ❀

What is the first thing that comes to mind when you hear the words
Exodus and Moses? What, if anything, does this have to do with Jesus?

Participants' answers will vary.

How was Jesus' early life similar to that of Moses?

As young children, Jesus and Moses both faced mortal danger
from their rulers.

How does Passover relate to Holy Communion?

During Passover, worshipers ate the meat, that is, the body of
the Passover lamb. In Holy Communion, we eat the body and
drink the blood of Jesus Christ, the Lamb of God, who takes
away the sin of the world.

What offer did Moses make to turn God's anger from Israel?

He pleaded with the Lord to blot his own name out of God's
book in exchange for saving Israel.

How was the tabernacle a foreshadowing of Jesus?

God dwelt among His people in the tent of meeting, or
tabernacle.

What is the connection between the mercy seat and the ark of
the covenant?

The mercy seat was the lid that covered the ark of the covenant.

What was the symbolism behind this sacrifice?

Don't focus on the specific animal being sacrificed but on the
fact that this sacrifice was taking place continuously. No matter
what time of year, day or night, you would find an offering
burning on the altar. This powerfully portrays the fact that the
fires of hell last eternally.

Why did God set such strict rules for how the high priest could approach His presence on the Day of Atonement?

> Aaron and all his descendants were sinners, like you and me. That made them unworthy to stand in God's presence. God used the sacrifice of animals to indicate that no sinner could approach God unless God's Son died for their sins and covered them with His blood.

How did Aaron and his sons, the line of high priests in Israel, foreshadow Jesus Christ?

> They brought the blood of sacrificial animals into the Lord's presence to win forgiveness for Israel's sins. On the cross, Jesus brought His own blood into the Father's presence to win forgiveness for the sins of all people of all time.

How did the live goat point ahead to Jesus Christ?

> This scapegoat of the Old Testament pointed ahead to Jesus' Baptism. After His Baptism, John the Baptist pointed to Him and said, "Behold, the Lamb of God, who takes away the sins of the world!" (John 1:29). When John the Baptist laid his hand on Jesus' head, Jesus took up all the sins washed away in our Baptism. He would carry them to the cross at Calvary.

What part of our worship service is most meaningful for you?

> Participants' answers will vary.

Describe an opportunity you lost because you were filled with fear or doubt.

> Participants' answers will vary.

How does the serpent on the pole foreshadow Jesus' mission?

> Just as the serpent was raised up and hung on the pole, Jesus would be raised up and hung on the cross. All who trusted God's promise to forgive them for Jesus' sake would be saved by faith.

Name a great work of God in the Bible that gives you comfort and confidence when you face difficulties.

Participants' answers will vary.

How does this passage fit with Jesus' forty days of fasting in the wilderness?

God the Father was humbling Jesus and testing Him to see where He put His trust, especially when He was very hungry.

How was Jesus' situation on the peak of the temple similar to Israel's experience at Massah?

In both cases, the question was raised: could God's people trust Him? Satan wanted Jesus to prove His trust in His Father by recklessly throwing Himself down. Jesus knew that Israel should have quietly trusted God and pleaded with Him to keep them and their livestock from dying of thirst.

How did Jesus use this passage to resist Satan's shortcut?

Satan was offering Jesus an easy way to bypass the cross and get the glory God promised Him. Jesus remembered these words and knew it was only by serving the Father that He could save humanity and please God, His Father.

How does this promise relate to Jesus?

Jesus was the ultimate prophet, like Moses.

How does this passage point ahead to Jesus?

Jesus was put to death on a tree, the cross. Hanging on that tree and carrying our sins, Jesus was cursed.

What new thing have you learned from this section that helps you better understand Jesus as He is presented in the Old Testament?

Participants' answers will vary.

❀ SESSION 3 ❀

Why is Rahab's presence in the line of Jesus so important?

It reminds us that Jesus came among sinners and identified with us so He could save us from those sins.

Who was this man?

Most will say an angel. But we will investigate the hints the text gives us.

What great miracles did God work? Why?

God hurled huge stones from heaven—that is, hail—and made the sun stand still in the sky so the Israelites could defeat their enemies, who would have escaped in the darkness otherwise.

Why was Gideon an unlikely judge?

He was a timid man, skeptical that God would deliver Israel.

How did Samson free Israel from their captivity to the Philistines?

At his death, Samson killed all the rulers and nobles of the Philistine city states. Basically, he destroyed the government of Philistia.

What is a redeemer?

A redeemer is someone who buys back someone or something.

Why is the Book of Ruth important enough to be in the Bible?

Ruth was in the ancestral line that led to King David.

What promise did Hannah make to the Lord regarding her son?

She would dedicate him to the Lord's service all his life.

How was Hannah's prayer similar to Mary's song in Luke 1:46–55?

Both Hannah and Mary spoke of the same theme: God exalting the humble and humbling the proud by using His mighty power to benefit the poor and lowly.

How are verses 19–20 similar to Luke 2:52, "And Jesus increased in wisdom and in stature and in favor with God and man"?

From their youth, it was obvious that both Samuel and Jesus would be powerful men of God, men God would use to richly bless His people.

How was Samuel unique among the judges?

All the judges were leaders of Israel, but only Samuel served Israel in all three offices of prophet, priest, and judge.

What was so bad about Saul offering the sacrifice, since Samuel was late?

Saul lost faith and didn't trust Samuel or God.

How does David's battle against Goliath foreshadow Jesus' battle with Satan?

David seemed unlikely to defeat Goliath, having no armor and carrying nothing but a sling and some stones. Jesus seemed even more unlikely, carrying nothing but His cross.

How was David's experience with Saul's jealousy similar to what Jesus later experienced?

Jesus suffered similar persecution from the Jewish religious leaders, who were jealous of Him and hunted after Him, seeking to kill Him.

What did the people mean when they said, "When Saul was king over us, it was you who led out and brought in Israel" (v. 2)?

After his victory against Goliath, David became a commander in Israel's army and kept rising in rank until he was captain of Saul's bodyguard. He was the real leader of Israel's army, not Saul.

Of what event in Jesus' life might this entrance of the ark into Jerusalem remind us?

It reminds us of Jesus' triumphant entry into Jerusalem on Palm Sunday.

What is so important about this prophecy?

God was informing David that his descendant would be the promised Christ.

❁ SESSION 4 ❁

What was so significant about the temple?

Before the temple, God dwelt in a portable tent that traveled with Israel through the wilderness. Now that Israel was settled in the Promised Land, the temple was a permanent dwelling place where God's people could always come together to find Him.

How did Elijah point to Jesus?

In the last Old Testament book, Malachi, a prophecy is given: "Behold, I will send you Elijah the prophet before the great and awesome day of the LORD comes" (Malachi 4:5). Malachi was speaking of John the Baptist, who dressed and preached like Elijah did.

How did Elijah's manner of leaving the earth foreshadow Jesus' departure?

As Elisha watched, Elijah was taken up to heaven in a whirlwind, with horses and chariots of fire. Jesus also ascended into the sky, until a cloud hid Him from His disciples' watching eyes.

How did Elisha's miracles foreshadow Jesus?

God worked through Elisha to perform a few of the same kinds of miracles that Jesus later worked in great numbers.

How did God save Ahaziah's youngest son, Joash, and keep the line leading to Jesus intact?

His aunt Jehosheba hid him from Athaliah.

How did God save Jerusalem?

He sent a single angel, who killed 185,000 Assyrian warriors overnight.

Why was the release of King Jehoiachin important?

The line of Jesus ran through Jehoiachin and his descendants. If Jehoiachin had died childless in prison, it is likely the line leading to Christ would have died with him.

What connection might there be between David bringing the ark into Jerusalem and events in the life of Jesus?

The ark was the object in which God dwelt among His people. Jesus' physical body was like that ark, for in Jesus' physical body the fullness of God dwelt among His people.

How did this event foreshadow the sacrifice of Christ?

In verse 17, David said, "Please let Your hand, O LORD my God, be against me and against my father's house." When Jesus went to the cross, He carried the sins of the world, including David's census. God's hand was against Jesus, and He was punished in the place of David and each of us.

According to the chronicler, at what moment did the cloud of the Lord's glory fill the temple?

The cloud filled the temple when the priests and Levite musicians praised God.

What is so ironic about what Joash did to Zechariah, Jehoiada's son?

Joash had him stoned to death in the court of the temple, the same place where Zechariah's father had hidden him so many years before.

Why did Jesus include Zechariah with Abel here?

Both were believers who were put to death for their faith. In Genesis 4:10, God told Cain that Abel's blood was crying out to Him from the ground for vengeance; and Zechariah also asked the Lord to see and avenge his death.

What did such a faithless man like Ahaz have to do with Jesus?

He was part of the genealogical line leading to Jesus (Matthew 1:9). We are reminded that Jesus did not come from a spotless line, but from one that was full of both faithful and faithless men and women.

Of what event in Jesus' life does this cleansing of the temple remind us?

Jesus cleansed the temple of those selling sacrificial animals and exchanging money in the Gentile court.

How did this passage point to Jesus Christ?

Found at the end of the Hebrew Old Testament Bible, it announced the return to Jerusalem and rebuilding of the temple in anticipation of the coming of the promised Savior, Jesus Christ.

Why did the Jews rebuild the altar before they began rebuilding the temple?

The first step to serving God was to begin sacrificing offerings again. The returned exiles were seeking God's protection and help to rebuild the temple.

Why did King Artaxerxes decide to halt construction on the temple?

Historical records indicated that the city had been the source of sedition and rebellion in the past, and mighty kings from Jerusalem had ruled over that entire province.

How were Tattenai, the Persian governor, and Darius, the Persian king, crucial to the completion of the temple?

Unlike earlier officials, they could not be bribed, and they searched diligently for the truth. When the truth of Cyrus's decree was found, they enforced that decree.

What authority did the king give to Ezra?

He authorized Ezra to appoint magistrates and judges who knew the law of God, and to teach those officials who did not know it. Ezra had power to judge anyone who did not obey the law of God and the law of the Persian king.

What promises of God did Nehemiah claim in his prayer?

He claimed God's promises through Moses (found in Leviticus and Deuteronomy) to restore His people if they repented and called upon Him.

Which people opposed Nehemiah's work for Jerusalem and for God?

The most notable was Sanballat, who was likely the governor of Samaria. Probably afraid of losing his authority in the region, he was enraged when he learned of the work on Jerusalem's walls. Already the tension and prejudice between Jews and Samaritans was great. Now this opposition increased it dramatically.

What was so dangerous about this plot?

Not only would it kill an entire people, but it would also exterminate the line leading to the promised Savior.

What did Mordecai mean when he said, "Relief and deliverance will rise for the Jews from another place" (v. 14)?

Mordecai was convinced God would faithfully preserve the line leading to Christ. He reminded Esther that God likely put her in that position so that as queen, she could appeal to her husband and have the plot foiled.

❈ SESSION 5 ❈

How would you describe Job's position before troubles befell him?

Job was a kindly man who feared God and was a good neighbor to all the people.

How do you think Job was able to answer in faith rather than in hurt and anger?

Job walked with God. He had a wonderful grasp on the nature of life—that his earthly life was short and when that life came to an end, he would leave this world taking nothing with him; but through the coming Messiah, he would be raised to eternal life.

Who were the "foolish women" Job mentioned to his wife?

In the Bible, a "fool" is one who has no faith or trust in God. Job was watching out for his wife's faith here. In her great grief at the loss of her children, she struggled with anger toward God. Job was cautioning her not to be among those who had no faith and trust in God, but to instead find her hope and peace in God.

What indirect accusation did Eliphaz make?

Eliphaz was trying to be gentle with Job. He did not want to directly come out and say that Job had committed a sin for which he was being punished, but he implied that was the case. He hoped Job would take the hint and repent.

How does this passage point to Jesus Christ?

Jesus is the God-man who mediates between God and sinners.

What is remarkable about this prophecy?

Job declared what God would accomplish in the future: our Lord Jesus' resurrection and His return to judge and restore the world on the Last Day.

How might this experience have influenced David's thoughts about Israel's worship?

David might have noticed how songs of praise and worship drove the evil spirit away from Saul. Godly music would likewise be a powerful tool for the children of God in worship.

How is this similar to Judas's betrayal of Jesus?

Absalom took advice from David's trusted counselor, Ahithophel. Like Judas, who ate and drank with Jesus as one of the Twelve, Ahithophel ate and drank at David's table, then betrayed him into Absalom's hands. Interestingly, in 2 Samuel 17:1–3, Ahithophel advised Absalom to let him select a special military team that would kill David alone, just as Judas singled out Jesus with a kiss. Ahithophel hung himself when Absalom did not take his advice, and Judas hung himself when he saw that Jesus was condemned.

How can Jesus be both David's Lord and David's son?

Jesus is David's Lord because He is the eternal Son of God, but Jesus is David's son because He became man and was born of David's descendant, the Virgin Mary.

How might this passage remind us of Jesus' public ministry?

Jesus went from village to village, teaching people about confessing their sins, trusting in His salvation, and living in the kingdom of God.

Why is it important to remember Jesus' role in creating the world?

Christ is our Creator, together with the Father and the Holy Spirit. He is the Word through which God made all things. Because Adam and Eve sinned, Jesus became human and came to restore us, and He will return on the Last Day to perfectly restore His creation.

How does the advice of Solomon fit with Jesus' parable of the rich fool in Luke 12:16–21?

Both speak about the worthlessness of spending all our effort to satisfy our pleasures or of building up our earthly treasures instead of seeking God's kingdom and finding joy in the simple blessings He gives each day.

What is the danger of waiting to repent until later in our life?

We have no guarantee that we will live to see tomorrow—or even the next hour. People die suddenly and unexpectedly every day. *Today* is the day to repent of our sins and receive God's forgiveness for Jesus' sake.

What event involving Jesus did Solomon speak of here?

After showing the emptiness of life without God, Solomon reminded each of his readers that eventually they will die and find themselves standing before Christ on Judgment Day, when the Lord will judge every deed—even those we think are secret.

What does the phrase "His banner over me was love" mean?

Armies usually carried banners, or standards, which guided the warriors. To the community members watching the armies marching past them to war, these banners indicated protection. Like armies carrying their banners, Jesus carried His cross to Calvary. His cross—His "banner"—is the clear demonstration of His love for us, and it reminds us of the battle He won against Satan to protect and defend us from sin, death, and hell.

What does it mean to say, "Love is strong as death" (v. 6)?

Death holds power over all humanity. No matter how great and powerful any emperor, king, or prophet is, none can overpower death. But God's love is more than a match for death.

❈ SESSION 6 ❈

What kinds of sins would have turned the hands of the Israelites scarlet and crimson?

> In verse 15, God mentions that their hands were full of blood. It can easily remind us of the sin of murder, bloodshed.

How was this prophecy of Christ's virgin birth a sign to Ahaz?

> It gave Ahaz a time frame within which God would permit Assyria to conquer Israel and Syria but then drive the Assyrians out of Judah.

Why does this prophecy mention "the throne of David" (v. 7)?

> In 2 Samuel 7:11–12, God promised to build David a "house"— with a Son who would be the Messiah who would reign over Israel forever.

Why is Jesus described as a shoot coming forth from the stump of Jesse?

> He was the descendant of Jesse's son David who became King of Israel and all creation.

What mountain was Isaiah speaking of where God would make "a feast of rich food" for all peoples?

> He spoke of Mount Calvary, the place where Jesus was crucified. In Jesus' death, He destroyed death, and in His resurrection, He guaranteed our own on the Last Day.

Of what person does this prophecy speak?

> This prophecy speaks of the ministry of John the Baptist. In fact, he used this very passage to identify himself when the chief priests from Jerusalem sent priests to ask who he was and what he had to say about himself.

Which action in Isaiah's prophecy grasps you the most?

Answers will vary, but each action reveals Jesus' amazing humility as He concerns Himself with fulfilling His Father's will and saving Israel, not His own glory and recognition.

On what aspect of Jesus' sacrifice did Isaiah center this prophecy?

Isaiah especially focused on the exchange that would take place on the cross. Jesus would take our guilt upon Himself and give us His own righteousness through faith. He would be stricken, smitten, and afflicted by God for the offenses *we* have committed.

What words in this passage prophesy Jesus' resurrection?

These words in verse 10, "He shall see His offspring; He shall prolong His days," speak of Christ's resurrection.

Why is Jesus called a "Branch"?

As noted earlier, the Bible often compares kingdoms and dynasties with large growing trees. When Babylon conquered Jerusalem, its emperor deposed and imprisoned the king from the line of David. It was as if the tree of David had been cut down and only a dead stump remained. Then, centuries later, when God's time was right, a shoot—or branch—sprouted out of that stump: Jesus of Nazareth.

How does this passage help us understand Jesus' prayer in the Garden of Gethsemane, "My Father, if it be possible, let this cup pass from Me; nevertheless, not as I will, but as You will" (Matthew 26:39)?

Jesus was using this cup imagery from Jeremiah to describe the suffering He would endure on the cross as He suffered God's wrath for every sin of all mankind. We can think of Jesus trying to carry the cross, staggering, stumbling, and falling beneath its weight.

What does the phrase "like Shiloh" (vv. 6, 9) mean?

Shiloh was the place where the tabernacle and the ark of the covenant were located after the Promised Land was conquered. Shiloh was later overrun and destroyed by the Philistines.

How does the treatment of Jeremiah in this passage remind us of what Jesus suffered?

The Jewish authorities laid hands on Jesus when their soldiers arrested Him in the Garden of Gethsemane. They tried Him and declared that He should be put to death.

Who was Rachel?

Rachel was Jacob's beloved wife.

In connection with what event in Jesus' childhood did Matthew use this passage?

In Matthew 2:18, this passage is connected with the murder of the little boys of Bethlehem two years old and younger by King Herod in an attempt to exterminate the Messiah after the Wise Men did not return to him with Jesus' location.

What was Jeremiah predicting in these words?

When Jesus completed His work on the cross and sent the Holy Spirit at Pentecost, God's new covenant with His people would be in place, fulfilling Jeremiah's words.

What was Jeremiah teaching us about Jesus?

He was teaching us that Jesus is a King who executes justice and righteousness and grants peace and security to all His people.

How does this passage apply to Jesus' crucifixion?

On Good Friday, God the Father bound all our transgressions together and laid them on Jesus, and He poured out His fierce anger at those sins onto Jesus.

How can this passage remind us of Jesus' life?

Jesus' body was the true temple of the Lord, the Son of God dwelling in His physical body. In His death, that temple of the Lord was crushed like a flimsy hut.

What did Jesus mean by "the time of your visitation"?

He meant the time God's Son visited it and preached repentance and faith but the leaders and people of Jerusalem refused to repent and believe.

❊ SESSION 7 ❊

How could this passage apply to Jesus, who is without sin?

Jesus took our sins upon Himself as our substitute and, bearing our sins, He suffered the punishment we deserve on the cross.

What did Ezekiel mean when he wrote, "A ruin, ruin, ruin I will make it," and, "This also shall not be" (v. 27)?

He was speaking of the house of David, that is, the offspring of David ruling as kings over the people of Judah. Judah's last king, Zedekiah, broke a treaty he had made with Nebuchadnezzar, king of Babylon. The Babylonian armies returned and laid siege to Jerusalem. When it fell, Zedekiah was blinded and dragged off to Babylon, where he died. Judah ceased to be a kingdom, and no Jewish kings rose to rule over it until Christ Jesus came.

What was the significance of a horn in the Old Testament?

In the Old Testament, the horn (like the horn of a power-ful animal such as a bull) was a symbol for great power and strength.

How did this comfort the exiles? How can it comfort us?

The exiles were far from home, scattered on the day of Judah's fall. God promised in the person of His Son to come as our Shepherd to seek and find them, no matter where they had been scattered.

Who is God's "servant David," who would be king over His united people?

This refers to "David's son," his descendant Jesus Christ.

What does the water flowing from the temple symbolize?

> In the Old Testament, water often symbolized life. Here it shows the new, eternal life that flows from the Savior, the promised Messiah.

Who is the stone that destroyed these kingdoms?

> The "stone" is Jesus Christ and His kingdom, the Holy Christian Church.

Who is the "Ancient of Days" (v. 9)?

> This "Ancient of Days" is God the Father. Jesus is the "one like a son of man" in verse 13, who came to the Ancient of Days and was presented before Him.

Where is Jesus in this mysterious passage?

> Jesus is the "anointed one" (v. 25), the prince who would be "cut off" (crucified) and have nothing in verse 26.

❀ SESSION 8 ❀

Where do we see Jesus in this passage?

The Lord spoke of Himself as the Husband, pointing to Jesus'
relationship with the Church, His Bride.

Where do we see Jesus' resurrection?

Verse 2 says, "After two days He will revive us; on the third
day He will raise us up." Jesus was raised from the dead on the
third day.

How does a booth represent Jesus Christ?

A lowly booth does a good job of characterizing Jesus' ministry.
He did not live or dress like a royal prince or king in his palace,
but as a poor, homeless preacher traveling from place to place
throughout Israel.

How can we see Jesus in this passage?

Jesus suffered the same hatred and hostility from His enemies
that the Jews experienced from the Edomites.

How were their experiences similar?

Both were sleeping in a boat through a storm. Both were awak-
ened by frightened sailors. Both spoke words of God that stilled
the storm. In both cases, the sailors praised God after the waters
grew calm. Jonah was thrown into the sea and swallowed by a
large fish; Jesus was "swallowed" by the tomb. After three days,
Jonah emerged from the fish when it spat him out; Jesus emerged
from the tomb, resurrected.

*What was the difference between Jonah's reaction and Jesus'
reaction?*

> Jonah despised the people of Nineveh and was angry when they
> repented and God spared them. Jesus deeply loved the people
> of Jerusalem and wept over their refusal to repent and believe,
> and He mourned over the devastation they would bring upon
> themselves.

What is so important about this prophecy of Jesus' birthplace?

> The chief priests quoted this very passage, which led the Wise
> Men to be able to find Jesus when they followed His star
> (Matthew 2).

How can verse 15 apply to Jesus?

> He walked the mountains of Galilee and Judea, proclaiming
> the Good News of forgiveness and peace, since the kingdom of
> heaven was at hand.

How can this passage remind us of Jesus?

> Habakkuk was complaining about the injustice in Jerusalem.
> Jesus suffered that same injustice from the Jews.

*In the midst of great poverty and suffering, how could the prophet
find joy and peace?*

> The prophet could experience God's perfect peace—even joy—
> by trusting His promises through the far greater suffering of His
> Son, our Lord and Savior, Jesus Christ.

How does this passage foreshadow Jesus' death on the cross?

> The wrath, distress, anguish, darkness, and gloom in verse 15
> were definitely in evidence as Jesus was crucified for us, facing
> our Judgment Day for us as He received the punishment and
> wrath we deserve for our sins.

What does this passage tell us about the effects of Jesus' work on His Church?

We are the humble, lowly people of whom Zephaniah spoke. Jesus drives away our fear and quiets us with His love.

Why did this new temple seem like nothing to many of the old priests, Levites, and leaders of fathers' houses?

They remembered the opulent first temple, which Solomon had built. To them, this new temple would never match the beauty and elegance of Solomon's temple.

What does this passage reveal about the work of Jesus Christ?

In a single day, Good Friday, Jesus would suffer the punishment for all iniquities on earth, winning forgiveness for all people.

What event from Jesus' life was Zechariah prophesying?

Zechariah was speaking about Jesus' triumphal entry into Jerusalem on the Sunday before He died on the cross on Good Friday.

Which details of Judas's betrayal did Zechariah prophesy?

He told the exact sum of money paid to Judas to betray Jesus, how Judas threw these silver pieces into the temple in repentance, and how the priests then paid the money to a potter to buy a burial ground for strangers.

What events from Jesus' Passion was Zechariah prophesying?

He was prophesying that the Roman soldiers would pierce Jesus' hands and feet with nails and His side with a spear.

Who were the two messengers Malachi mentions?

The first messenger, "My messenger," was John the Baptist, Jesus' messenger. The second, "the messenger of the covenant," was Jesus Christ Himself.

Whom did Malachi mean by "Elijah the prophet"?

Jesus interpreted this prophecy as referring to John the Baptist.